Kites on the Wind

Easy-to-Make Kites

That Fly without Sticks

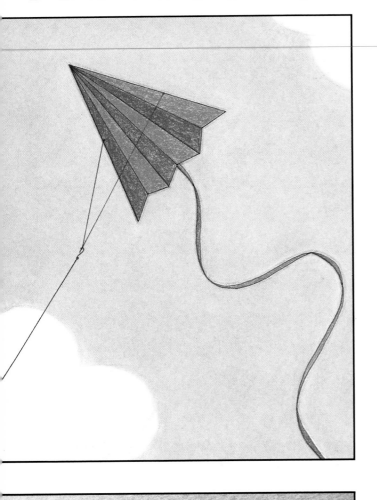

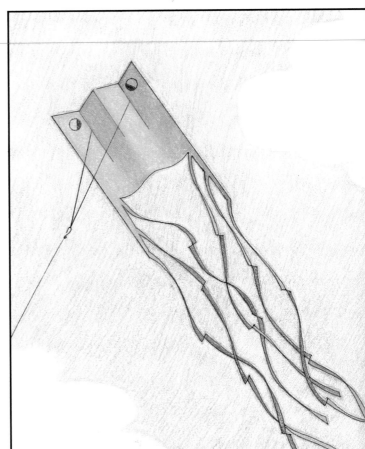

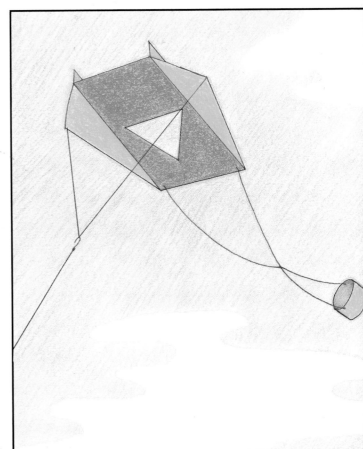

Kites on the Wind

Easy-to-Make Kites That Fly without Sticks

Emery J. Kelly

illustrations by Jennifer Hagerman

Lerner Publications Company ▪ Minneapolis

Dedicated to my wife, Janet, who was patient while I experimented with and flew the many versions of the kites in this book. She then acted as my first reader. She followed the first draft of the instructions, made the kites, and helped make this book more clear and understandable. Thanks, Dear!

Library of Congress Cataloging-in-Publication Data

Kelly, Emery J.
    Kites on the wind : easy-to-make kites that fly without sticks /
Emery J. Kelly.
      p.   cm.
      Summary: Provides instructions for making thirteen kinds of kites
that fly without sticks. Includes diagrams and flying tips.
      ISBN 0-8225-2400-7
    1. Kites—Juvenile literature. [1. Kites. 2. Handicraft.]
I. Title.
TL759.5.K35   1991
629.133′32—dc20
                              91-7364
                              CIP
                              AC

Manufactured in the United States of America

1 2 3 4 5 6 7 8 9 10 00 99 98 97 96 95 94 93 92 91

CONTENTS

In writing this book, I wanted to design a series of kites that were inexpensive and easy to build. You can make most of them out of a single sheet of 8½-by-11-inch paper, some tape, and some sewing thread. They have no frames or sticks—the folds in the paper provide the necessary stiffness.

To build your kites you'll need some simple household tools including a pencil, a ruler, and a pair of scissors or a sharp artist's knife. Because these kites require so few materials, you can make them any time you wish. If you lose a kite in a tree, in just a few minutes, you can make a new one!

Most of the kites are made with an ordinary sheet of paper, but the kites don't have to be white. You can use colored paper and magic markers to decorate your kites any way you like. You'll have great fun watching your own handiwork and creativity flying high overhead on the end of a string.

The kites become more challenging as you work your way through the book. After you gain experience flying the first simple kites, you will be ready to go on to the more complex box kites. If you follow the building and flying instructions carefully, you will have hours of fun watching your kites dance in the wind. Happy Flying!

Construction

The best way to begin construction on each kite is to read through the instructions and look at the diagrams and patterns. You will notice several different kinds of lines:

A solid, dark line (————) shows where to make a *cut*.

A dashed line (— — — —) shows where to make a *fold*.

A short line at the end of a solid or dashed line (————┤) shows where to *stop* cutting or folding.

Blue lines with arrows show *measurements* in inches.

$$|\!\longleftarrow\!2''\!\longrightarrow\!|$$
$$\longrightarrow\!2''\!\longrightarrow\!| \qquad\qquad |\!\longleftarrow$$

Both examples tell you to make a measurement of two inches between the arrows.

▨ shows where you will put a piece of tape.

Remember to make all folds as straight and as sharp as you can. One way to do this is to start the fold along the straight edge of a ruler or a tabletop. Use your fingernail to complete the fold, making it as sharp as possible without tearing the paper. Sharp folds will give the kite the stiffness it needs to withstand the pressure of the wind.

Be accurate in your measurements. Begin each kite by drawing the pattern from the large diagram onto your 8½-by-11-inch sheet of paper. The measurements are given with the " symbol, which stands for inches. If you are using a metric ruler, multiply the inch measurements by 2.5 to find centimeters.

Follow the instructions and patterns carefully. Most kites should be symmetrical. That is, they will be the same size and shape on both sides of the centerline.

Your flying line can be made of light thread or fishing line. Eight-pound fishing line or "invisible" plastic mending thread work well, but any kind of light thread will do. You can make a flying line hook out of a simple paper clip. Open up the clip as shown and pinch the edges to make the shape shown below.

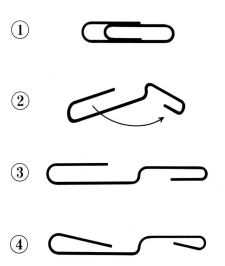

You will find that ordinary typing paper works well for most kites in the book. You may use other kinds of paper, but they shouldn't be too heavy or your kite will not fly very well. Stiff construction paper, for instance, might be too heavy.

What Makes Kites Fly

There are two principles of aerodynamics that explain what keeps kites in the air.

The first is Sir Isaac Newton's law of motion stating that for every action, there is an equal and opposite reaction. Study the diagram below. Note that as wind strikes the kite, the wind changes direction and flows downward (action). The reaction to this motion is that the kite moves upward, or lifts. The flying line keeps the kite from being dragged backward by the wind.

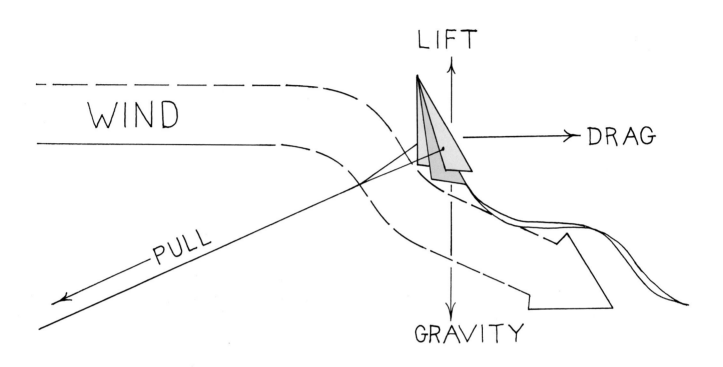

Another important aerodynamic principle is Daniel Bernuolli's discovery that as a fluid, such as air, moves faster, its pressure decreases. Cut a strip of paper, four inches wide, from the bottom of a sheet of typing paper. Fold a crease in the paper as shown in the diagram below. Now blow across it.

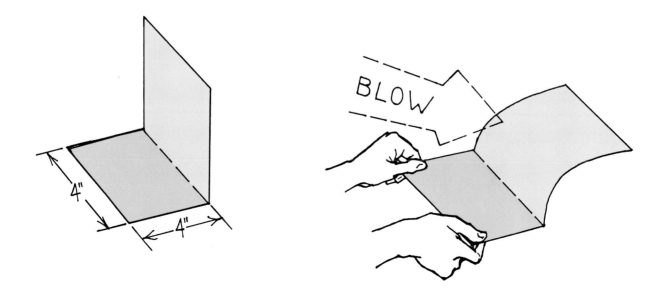

You will find that instead of forcing the paper down, your breath causes the paper to rise. The next diagram explains why. As wind passes over a kite (or your paper), the air on top must go farther than the air on the bottom, in the same amount of time. The air on top must speed up, and (as shown by Bernuolli's principle) this decreases pressure over the kite. Scientists also know that air will move from an area of high pressure toward an area of low pressure. As a result, the higher pressure air under the kite will push up, providing lift.

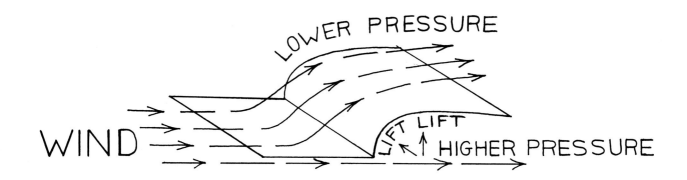

Kite Terms

The two diagrams below illustrate some terms you will need to know about the parts of a kite.

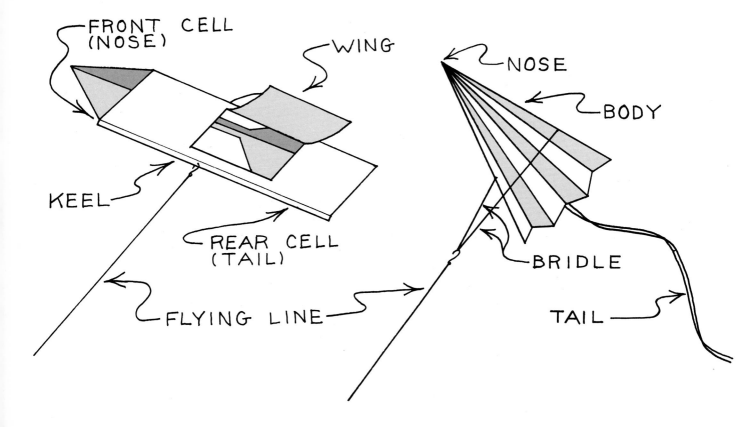

Flying Tips

• The best place to fly your kite is in a field without a lot of trees—trees cause low level turbulence (wind disturbance).

• The instructions for each kite include the best wind speed for that kite. You can estimate wind speed by observing the things around you:

WIND SPEED TABLE		
name of wind	miles per hour	observation
light breeze	1 - 3	smoke drifts
light wind	4 - 7	leaves rustle, wind vanes turn, light kites fly well
gentle wind	8 - 12	leaves and small twigs move constantly, small flags fly, most kites fly well
moderate wind	13 - 17	dust and papers fly, small branches move, only strong kites can fly well
fresh wind	18 - 24	small trees sway, kites in this book won't fly well in a fresh wind

• Stay far away from electric power lines, never fly a kite in wet or stormy weather, and never use line that contains metallic thread. You wouldn't want to repeat Benjamin Franklin's experiment proving that lightning is electricity.

• Winds 100 feet in the air will generally be stronger than winds near the ground, and they will usually blow from a different direction. You can get your kite aloft into these stronger winds by holding the flying line and walking backwards with your kite. This backward movement will make the forward force of the wind against your kite even greater.

• If the wind dies down suddenly, you can walk backward again to keep your kite up in the air. Reeling your flying line in will also work to increase the force of the wind against your kite. If the wind gusts and makes your kite circle, walking forward toward your kite or letting out more line will help stabilize it.

• Sometimes adjusting where the flying line is attached will change the way your kite flies. Usually, attaching the flying line toward the nose will help steady the kite. Moving the flying line toward the tail will increase lift, but will make your kite less stable.

• Winds 100 feet in the air will generally be stronger than winds near the ground, and they will usually blow from a different direction. You can get your kite aloft into these stronger winds by holding the flying line and walking backward with your kite. This backward movement will make the forward force of the wind against your kite even greater.

1 Adelino's Philippine Kite

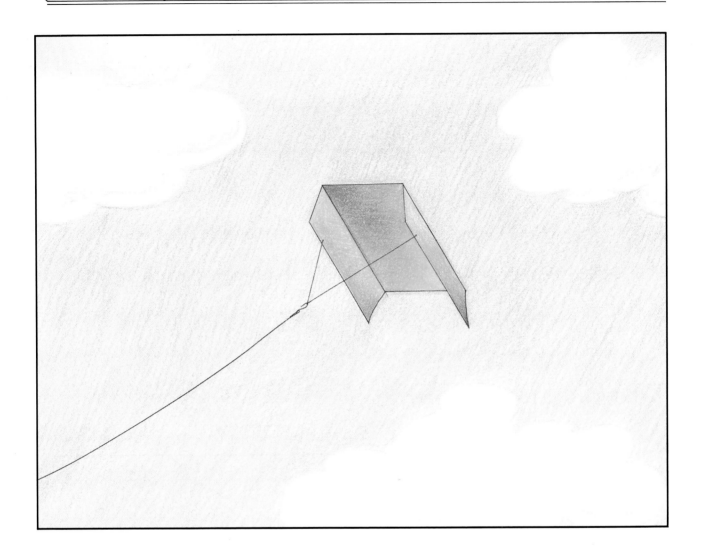

One day, as my friend Adelino and I discussed this book, he described a kite he had flown in the Philippines as a young boy. I tried the kite and found it was easy to make and fly. This kite flies without a tail.

Begin by drawing the fold and cut lines from the pattern on the opposite page onto your 8½-by-11-inch piece of paper. Use a ruler to make sure you have the correct measurements. The ″ sign means inches. If you are using a metric ruler, multiply the inch measurements by 2.5 to find centimeters.

Key to lines and symbols

A solid, dark line (————) shows where to make a *cut*.

A dashed line (— — — — —) shows where to make a *fold*.

A short line at the end of a solid or dashed line (————⊣) shows where to *stop* cutting or folding.

Blue lines with arrows show *measurements* in inches.

⊢←——2″——→⊣

————2″——→⊣   ⊢←

Both examples tell you to make a measurement of two inches between the arrows.

▨ shows where you will put a piece of tape.

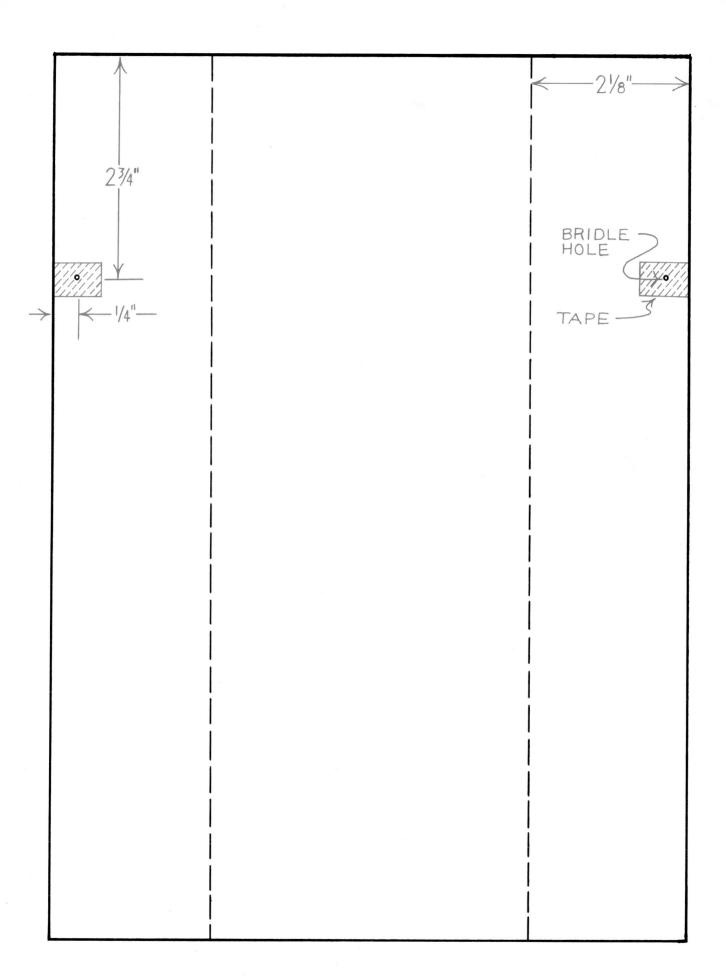

2¾"

2⅛"

¼"

BRIDLE
HOLE

TAPE

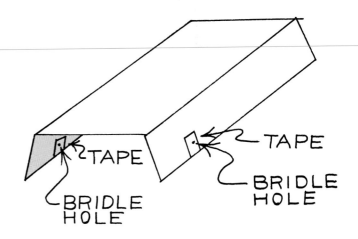

Make the two folds along the dashed lines, with the dashes inside the crease. Poke the bridle holes with a pin. You may want to reinforce the bridle holes with tape.

Cut a piece of thread 14 inches long to make the bridle. Tie one end of the bridle to each hole.

Make a hook out of a paper clip and tie your flying line to the hook.

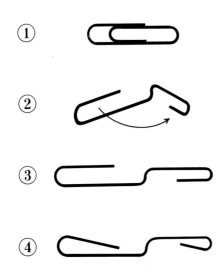

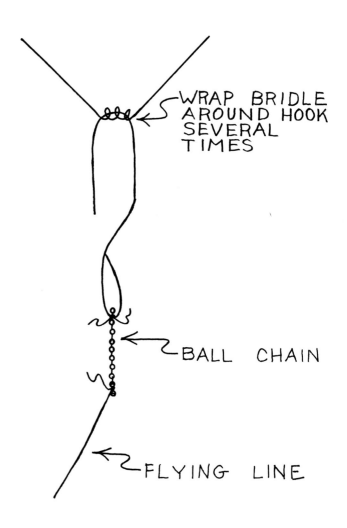

When making any of the kites in this book, you might want to tie a small piece of ball chain between the hook and the flying line. This will act as a "swivel" and keep the flying line from getting tangled. You can buy a piece of ball chain at a hardware store.

Attach the bridle to the flying line hook by wrapping the bridle around the hook three or four times. Make sure that both legs of the bridle are even.

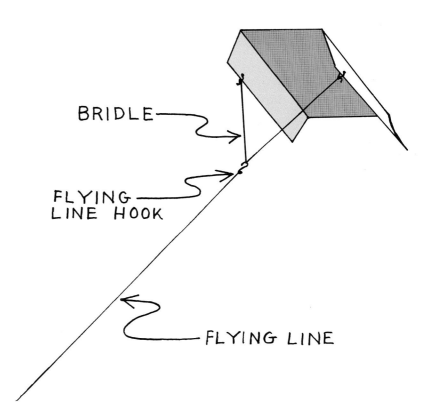

BRIDLE

FLYING
LINE HOOK

FLYING LINE

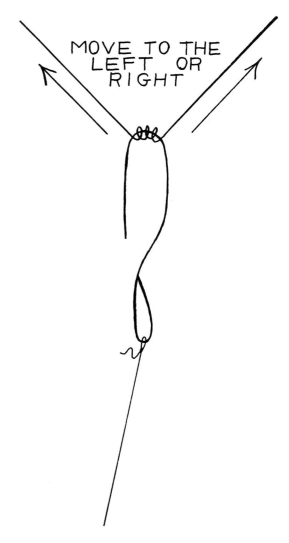

MOVE TO THE
LEFT OR
RIGHT

Follow the flying tips given on page 9. This kite flies well in light to moderate winds. If your kite seems to veer off to the right all of the time, move the flying line hook along the bridle so that the right bridle leg is longer than the left leg. If the kite veers to the left, make the left bridle leg longer. The hook should slide along the bridle with a bit of help.

After flying Adelino's kite, I wanted to make it fly even better. My kite has "sled runners" cut off at an angle near the nose. These help keep the kite's nose open in gusty winds.

The addition of "finger valves" in the body helps steady the kite in strong winds. These valves allow higher pressure air under the kite to mix with lower pressure air above the kite. This reduces turbulence.

Begin by drawing the fold and cut lines from the pattern on the opposite page onto your 8½-by-11-inch piece of paper. Use a ruler to make sure you have the correct measurements. The " sign means inches. If you are using a metric ruler, multiply the inch measurements by 2.5 to find centimeters.

Key to lines and symbols

A solid, dark line (————) shows where to make a *cut*.

A dashed line (— — — — —) shows where to make a *fold*.

A short line at the end of a solid or dashed line (————I) shows where to *stop* cutting or folding.

Blue lines with arrows show *measurements* in inches.

I←——2″——→I

————2″——→I   I←——

Both examples tell you to make a measurement of two inches between the arrows.

 shows where you will put a piece of tape.

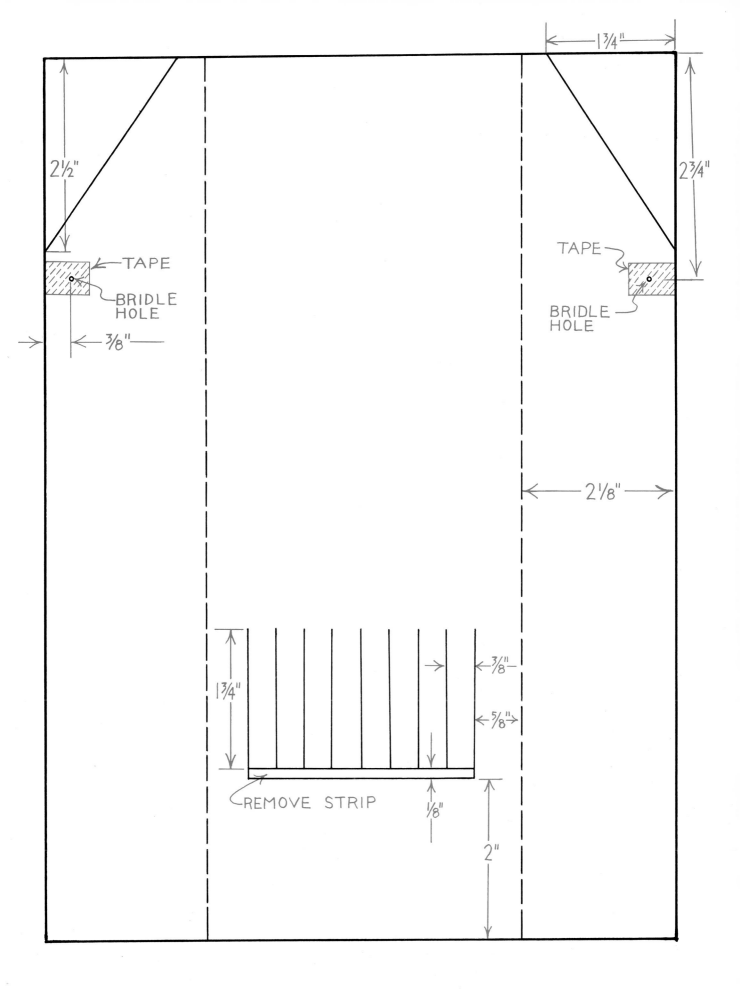

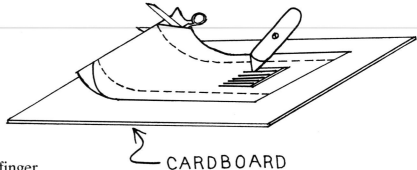

CARDBOARD

Cut out the sled runners and the finger valves as shown. A sharp artist's knife will help you make the finger valve cuts more easily. Whenever you use a sharp blade, be careful not to cut yourself, and be sure to protect your work surface with cardboard, a magazine, or a folded newspaper.

After you have cut out the finger valves, do not fold them. The force of the wind will make them open and close as necessary.

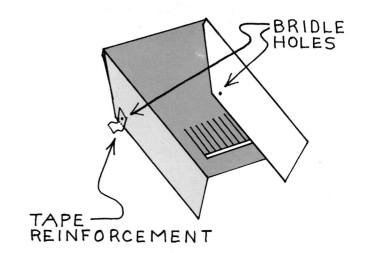

BRIDLE HOLES

Make the two folds along the dashed lines, with the dashes inside the crease. Reinforce the bridle holes with tape and poke the holes with a pin.

TAPE REINFORCEMENT

Tie a 14-inch piece of thread between the holes to form a bridle. Attach the flying line by wrapping the bridle around the hook three or four times and sliding the hook until both bridle legs are even.

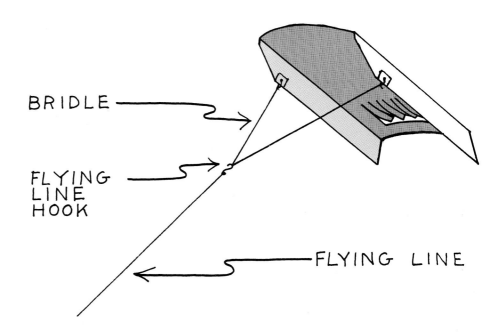

BRIDLE

FLYING
LINE
HOOK

FLYING LINE

This kite will fly well in light to moderate winds. If the kite veers to one side, adjust the flying line hook, as you did with Adelino's Kite, so that the bridle leg on that side is longer.

As the kite flies, watch how the finger valves move, adjusting to changes in wind pressure.

If you want to fly your kite in stronger winds, you will have to make the finger valves longer—four inches is about the limit. Experiment for the best flying results. You can make the fingers wider or narrower by changing the number of valves. If the valves are too long and narrow, however, they will bend sideways and tangle with one another.

Try making the Kelly Kite with a larger or smaller piece of paper. As you work your way through the kites in the book, you might want to experiment with different sizes and types of paper. Soon, you will be making up your own kite designs.

3 Arrow Kite

This kite is a good choice for beginners because it is easy to make and fly.

Begin by drawing the fold and cut lines from the pattern on the opposite page onto your 8½-by-11-inch piece of paper. Use a ruler to make sure you have the correct measurements. The ″ sign on the diagram means inches. If you are using a metric ruler, multiply the inch measurements by 2.5 to find centimeters.

Key to lines and symbols

A solid, dark line (————) shows where to make a *cut*.

A dashed line (— — — — —) shows where to make a *fold*.

A short line at the end of a solid or dashed line (————⊣) shows where to *stop* cutting or folding.

Blue lines with arrows show *measurements* in inches.

⊢←——2″——→⊣

———— 2″ ——→⊣   ⊢←

Both examples tell you to make a measurement of two inches between the arrows.

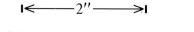 shows where you will put a piece of tape.

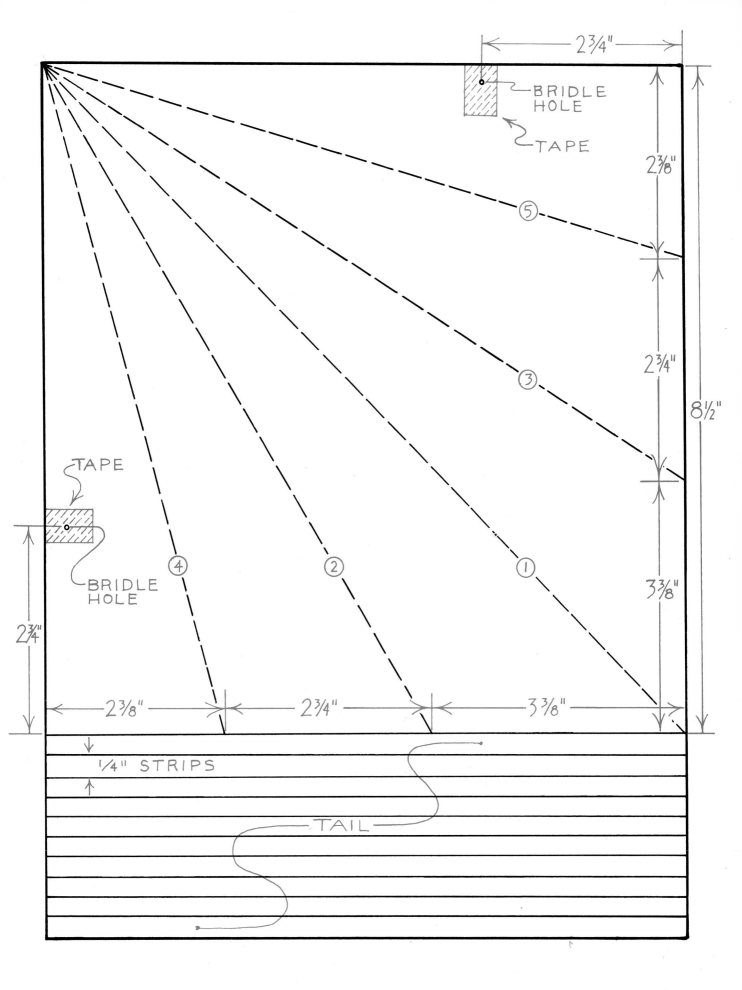

2¾"

BRIDLE
HOLE

TAPE

2⅜"

⑤

2¾"

③

8½"

TAPE

BRIDLE
HOLE

2¾"

④

②

①

3⅜"

2⅜"

2¾"

3⅜"

¼" STRIPS

TAIL

Make fold 1 with the dashed line inside the fold. Cut off the paper that extends below the fold. Set this piece aside to make the kite's tail.

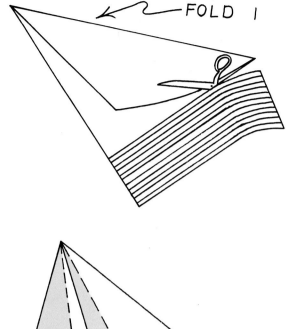

Make folds 2 and 3. These should be folded in the opposite direction from fold 1. The dashed lines should be on the outside crease of the folds.

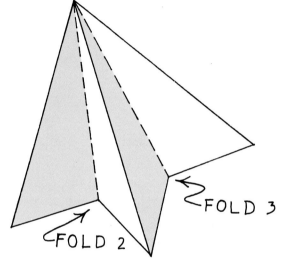

Finally, make folds 4 and 5. They should be the same as fold 1, with the dashed lines inside the creases.

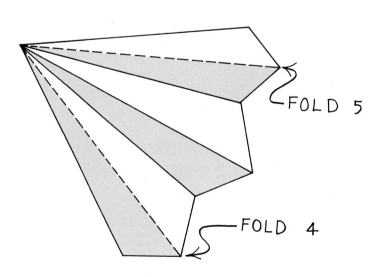

Cut the remaining piece of paper into ¼-inch strips. Tape the strips together to form the kite's tail. Tape the tail to the kite in the position shown.

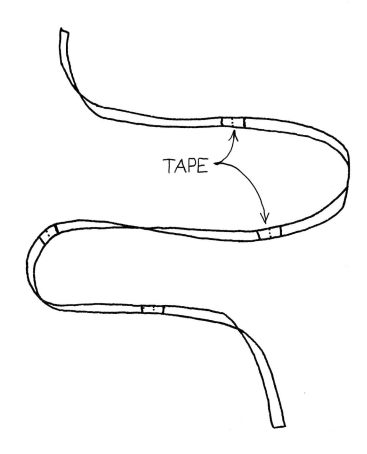

TAPE

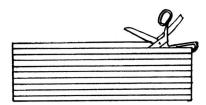

Place two pieces of tape over the bridle hole positions and poke the holes with a pin. The tape will reinforce the bridle holes.

The bridle is made of an 18-inch piece of thread tied from one of the bridle holes to the other. Loop the bridle thread three or four times around the flying line hook to attach the flying line. Adjust the bridle by sliding the hook until both legs are equal.

This kite flies in light to moderate winds. It should take off right from your hand. If the kite veers to one side or the other, adjust the flying line hook to make the bridle longer on that side.

If strong winds cause your kite to circle, increase the length of the kite's tail by adding more strips from a scrap piece of paper. A longer tail will steady your kite, but it will also increase drag, and your kite won't fly as high.

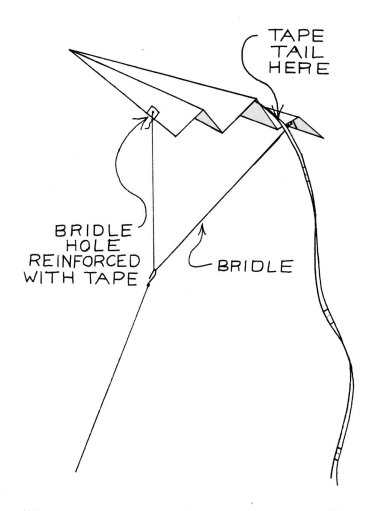

TAPE TAIL HERE

BRIDLE HOLE REINFORCED WITH TAPE

BRIDLE

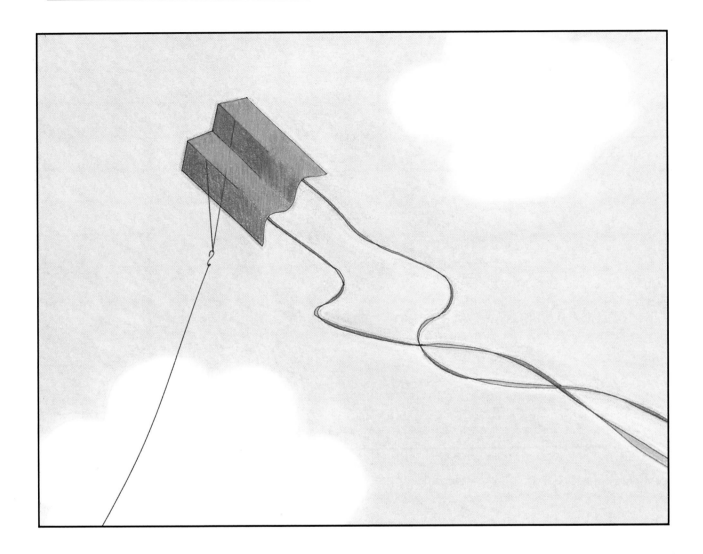

This W-shaped kite flies with twin tails and uses the unfolded part of the paper to stay open to the wind. Use a good bond paper to get the necessary stiffness.

Begin by drawing the cut and fold lines from the pattern on the opposite page onto your 8½-by-11-inch piece of paper. Use a ruler to make sure you have the correct measurements. The ″ sign means inches. If you are using a metric ruler, multiply the inch measurement by 2.5 to find centimeters.

Key to lines and symbols

A solid, dark line (———) shows where to make a *cut*.

A dashed line (— — — — —) shows where to make a *fold*.

A short line at the end of a solid or dashed line (———|) shows where to *stop* cutting or folding.

Blue lines with arrows show *measurements* in inches.

|←——2″——→|

———2″——→| |←

Both examples tell you to make a measurement of two inches between the arrows.

 shows where you will put a piece of tape.

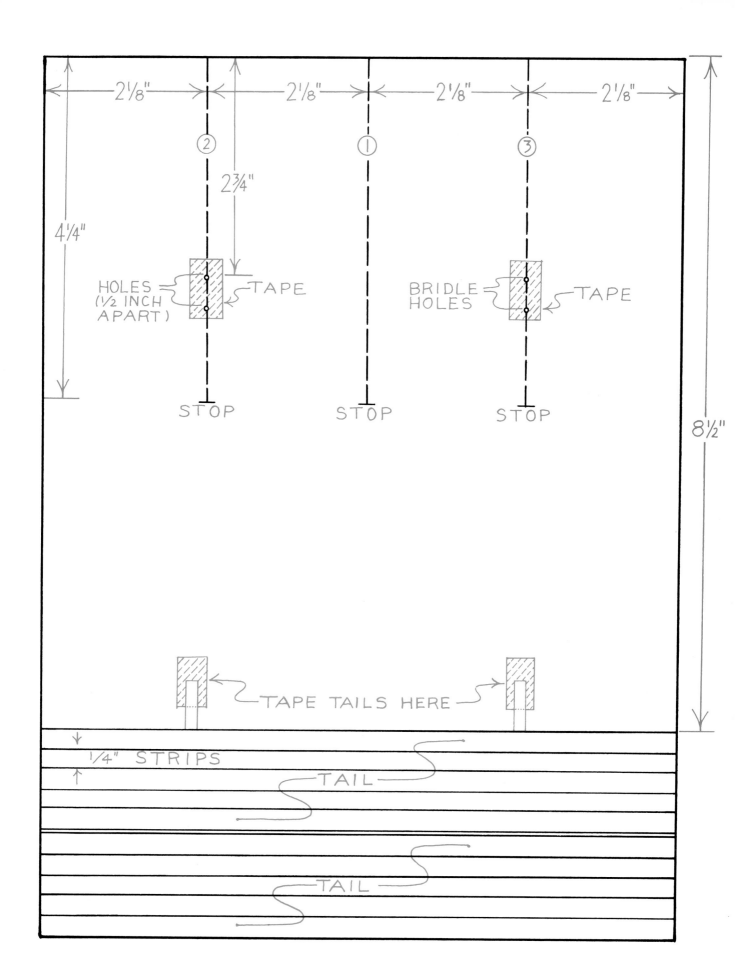

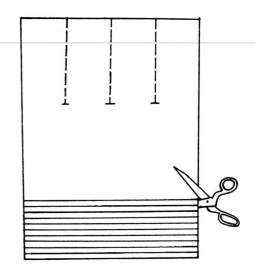

Cut off the bottom of the sheet marked "tail" and set it aside.

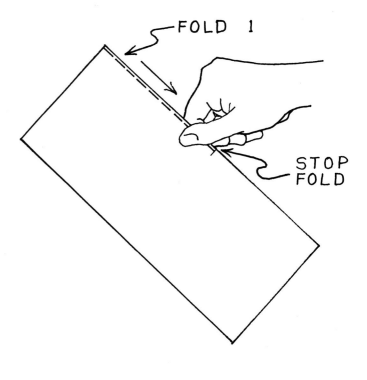

Make fold 1 with the dashed line outside the fold. Remember to stop the crease where the small line crosses the dashed line.

Make folds 2 and 3 so that the dashed line is on the inside of the crease. Stop at the small cross lines. These folds should be in the opposite direction from fold 1. The nose of the kite should form a W shape as shown in the drawing.

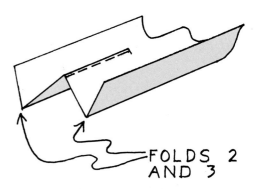

Take the remaining tail piece and cut it into ¼-inch strips. Tape these strips end-to-end to form two tails consisting of five strips each. Tape each tail to the kite as shown.

Place two pieces of tape on the inside of folds 2 and 3. Poke two bridle holes through each fold.

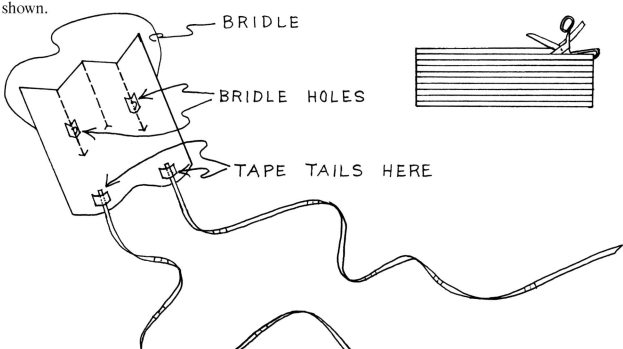

BRIDLE

BRIDLE HOLES

TAPE TAILS HERE

Form the bridle from an 18-inch piece of thread. Tie one end to the holes at fold 2. Pass the bridle around the bottom of the kite and tie the other end to the holes in fold 3.

Connect the flying line by wrapping the bridle around the flying line hook three or four times. Slide the hook along the bridle until the bridle legs are the same length.

The W Kite will fly in anything from a light breeze to a moderate wind. You will find that it flies overhead at a higher angle than does the Arrow Kite.

Make final adjustments as you did with the Arrow Kite. If the kite seems to fall off to one side, lengthen the bridle leg on that side until the kite flies evenly. If the kite circles in strong winds, lengthen the tails for more stability.

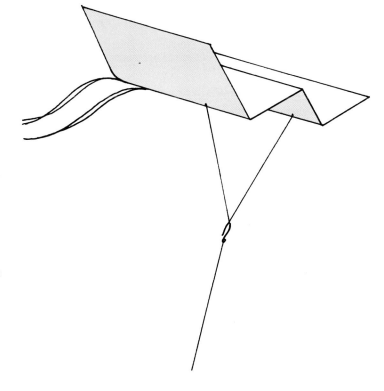

5 Chinese Kite

This kite is a good flyer and looks like a traditional Chinese kite. If you want to decorate your kite, you should use permanent, waterproof markers. Non-permanent markers have water in them that might cause your paper to wrinkle.

Begin by drawing the cut and fold lines from the pattern on the opposite page onto your 8½-by-11-inch piece of paper. Use a ruler to make sure you have the correct measurements. The ″ sign means inches. If you are using a metric ruler, multiply the inch measurement by 2.5 to find centimeters.

Key to lines and symbols

A solid, dark line (————) shows where to make a *cut*.

A dashed line (— — — — —) shows where to make a *fold*.

A short line at the end of a solid or dashed line (————|) shows where to *stop* cutting or folding.

Blue lines with arrows show *measurements* in inches.

|←———2″———→|

———— 2″ ———→| |←——

Both examples tell you to make a measurement of two inches between the arrows.

▨ shows where you will put a piece of tape.

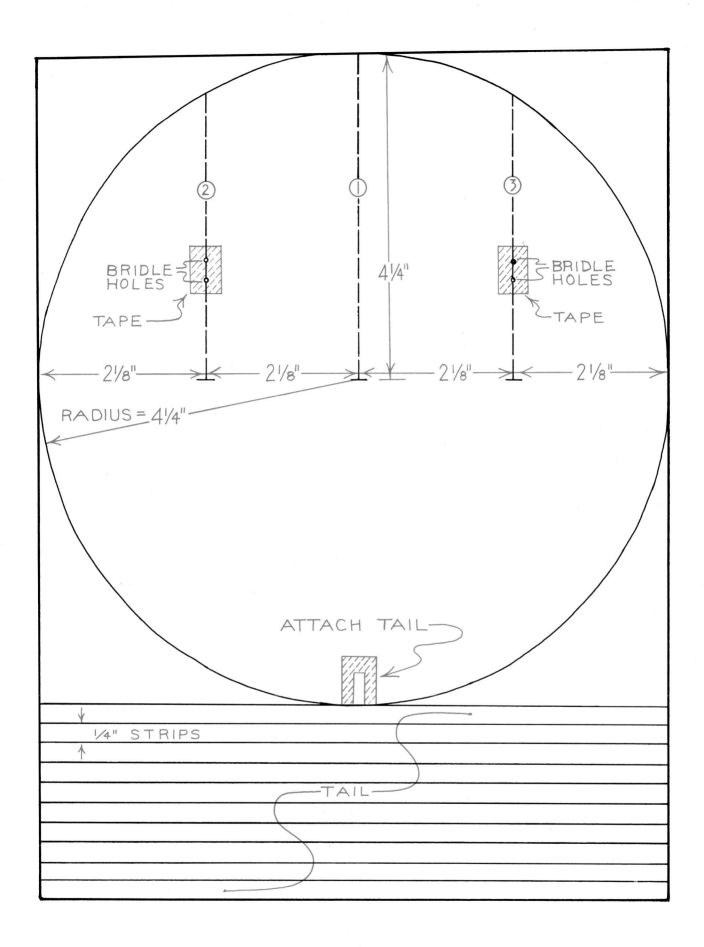

BRIDLE
HOLES

TAPE

②

①

③

BRIDLE
HOLES

TAPE

4¼"

2⅛" 2⅛" 2⅛" 2⅛"

RADIUS = 4¼"

ATTACH TAIL

¼" STRIPS

TAIL

Cut out the circular body of the kite and the piece at the bottom of your sheet marked "tail." Save the tail and the four corners that you cut from around the circle.

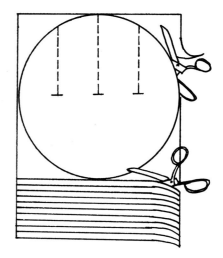

Make fold 1 with the dashed line on the inside of the crease. Make folds 2 and 3 with the dashed lines on the outside of the crease. Be sure the folds stop at the small cross lines.

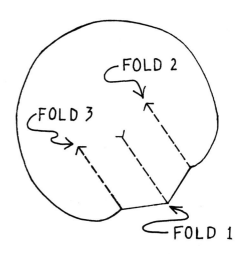

Cut the piece of paper marked "tail" into ¼-inch strips and tape those strips together into one long tail.

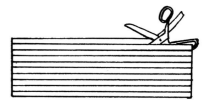

Fold the tail in half (the long way) and in half again. Straighten the tail out again.

Take the four corners that you cut from around the circle and tape them to the tail as shown. Put three of the corners on top of the creases and tape the fourth corner to the end of the tail.

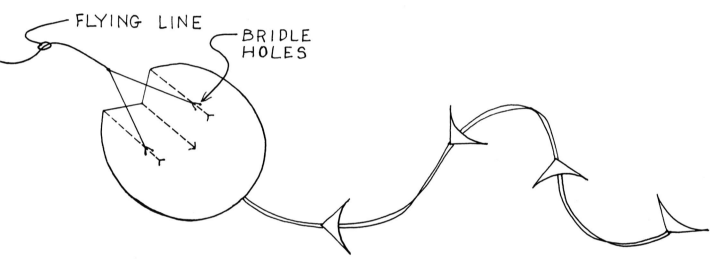

FLYING LINE

BRIDLE HOLES

Tape the tail to the body of the kite in the position marked on the pattern. Put two pieces of tape inside folds 2 and 3. Poke holes for the bridle with a pin.

Use an 18-inch piece of thread to form a bridle. Tie it from the holes in fold 2 to the holes in fold 3. Attach the flying line by wrapping the bridle thread around the flying line hook three times and sliding the hook until both legs of the bridle are equal.

This kite will fly well in light to moderate winds. Adjust the bridle legs and tail if necessary. This kite is a good steady flyer. You can decorate it with bright colors, and it will look great against the sky.

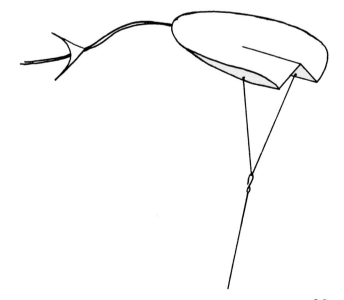

6 Octopus Kite

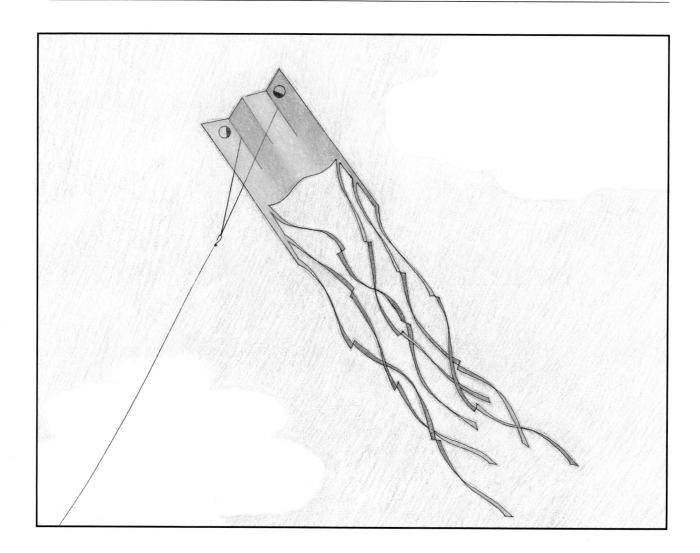

This kite has six tails that are cut from the body of the kite and stay attached. For this reason, the kite can be made without tape.

Begin by drawing the cut and fold lines from the pattern on the opposite page onto your 8½-by-11-inch piece of paper. Use a ruler to make sure you have the correct measurements. The ″ sign means inches. If you are using a metric ruler, multiply the inch measurements by 2.5 to find centimeters.

Key to lines and symbols

A solid, dark line (——————) shows where to make a *cut*.

A dashed line (— — — — —) shows where to make a *fold*.

A short line at the end of a solid or dashed line (——————⊣) shows where to *stop* cutting or folding.

Blue lines with arrows show *measurements* in inches.

⊢←———2″———→⊣

———2″———→⊣   ⊢←

Both examples tell you to make a measurement of two inches between the arrows.

▨ shows where you will put a piece of tape.

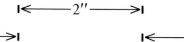

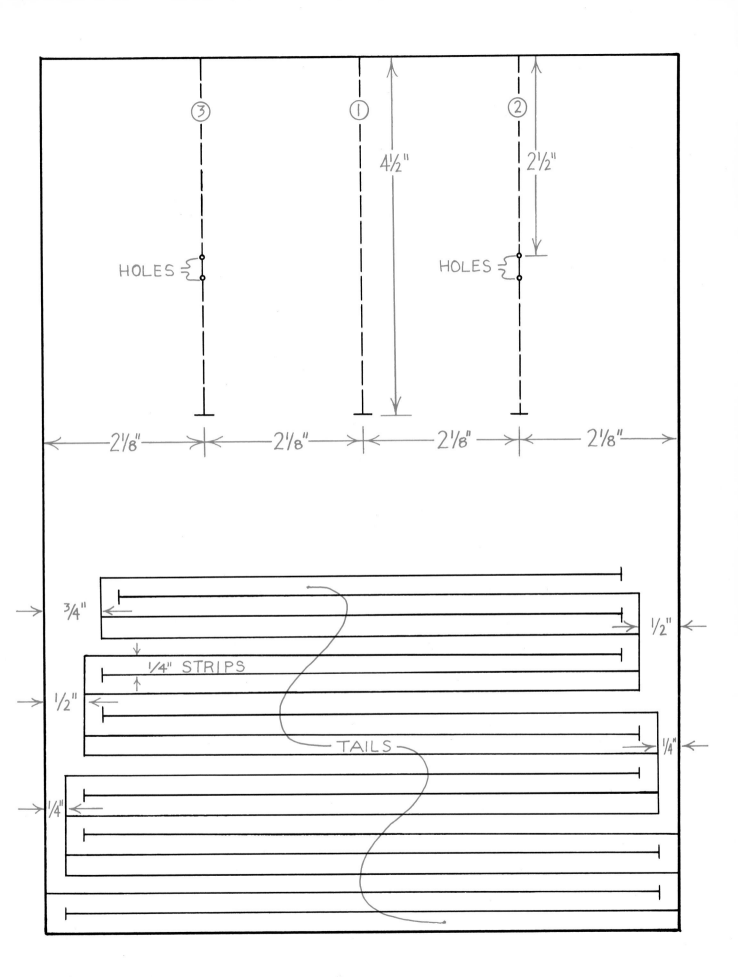

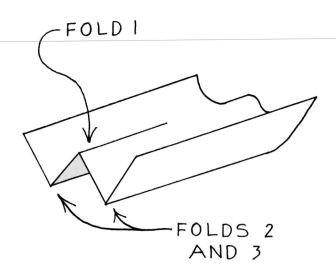

FOLD 1

FOLDS 2
AND 3

Fold this kite like the W kite. Start with fold 1 with the dashed line outside the crease. Make folds 2 and 3 in the opposite direction.

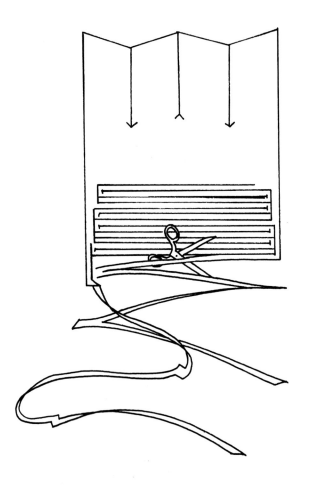

Starting at the bottom of the tail, make the first three cuts, stopping at the small cross lines. Notice that the three pieces form a long strip of paper that is still attached to the kite. Fold the strip so that it hangs down from the kite in a long line. Continue cutting each tail out, folding it down from the kite. If you make a mistake, fix it with a small piece of tape.

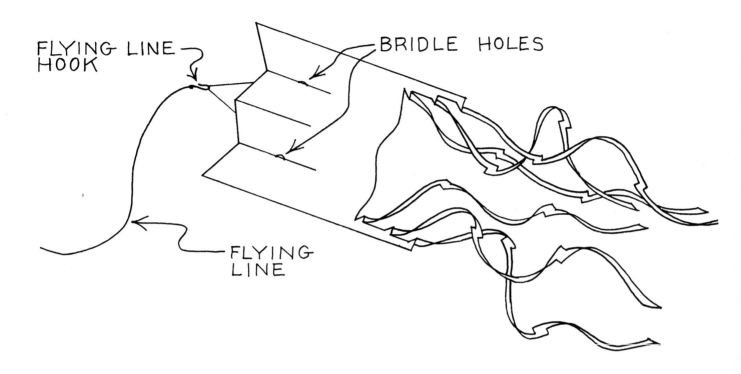

FLYING LINE HOOK

BRIDLE HOLES

FLYING LINE

Poke the four bridle holes in the kite as noted on the pattern. You may want to reinforce each hole with a piece of tape.

Attach an 18-inch piece of thread from the holes in fold 2 to the holes in fold 3. Attach the flying line by wrapping the bridle thread three times around the flying line hook. Slide the hook back and forth until each leg of the bridle is equal.

Decorate your kite like an octopus. The tails will look like tentacles in the sky.

The Octopus Kite will fly in light to moderate winds. You can make adjustments by sliding the flying line hook along the bridle.

7 Scott Sled Kite

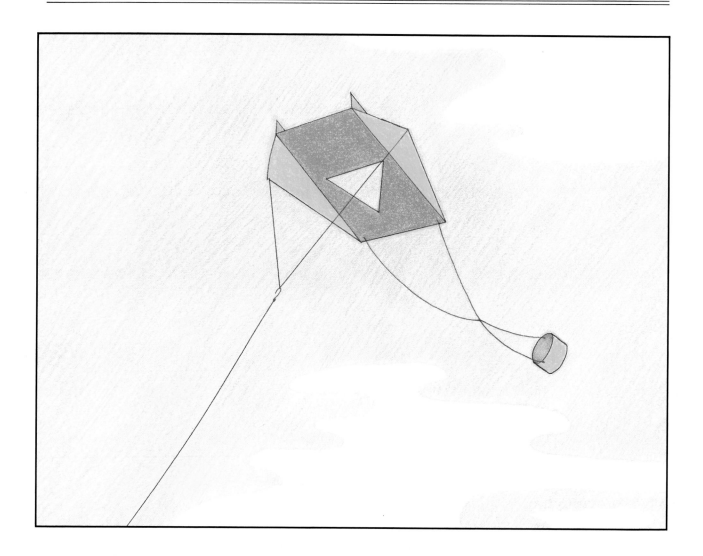

This kite was originally designed to fly without a tail. But, because it is so small, your kite will need a tail for stability. The ring-shaped tail you will make is called a "drouge" tail. It is different from any of the tails used so far.

Begin by drawing the cut and fold lines from the pattern on the opposite page onto your 8½-by-11-inch piece of paper. Use a ruler to make sure you have the correct measurements. The ″ sign means inches. If you are using a metric ruler, multiply the inch measurements by 2.5 to find centimeters.

Key to lines and symbols

A solid, dark line (————) shows where to make a *cut*.

A dashed line (— — — — —) shows where to make a *fold*.

A short line at the end of a solid or dashed line (————⊣) shows where to *stop* cutting or folding.

Blue lines with arrows show *measurements* in inches.

⊢←——— 2″ ———→⊣

————— 2″ ———→⊣   ⊢←

Both examples tell you to make a measurement of two inches between the arrows.

▨ shows where you will put a piece of tape.

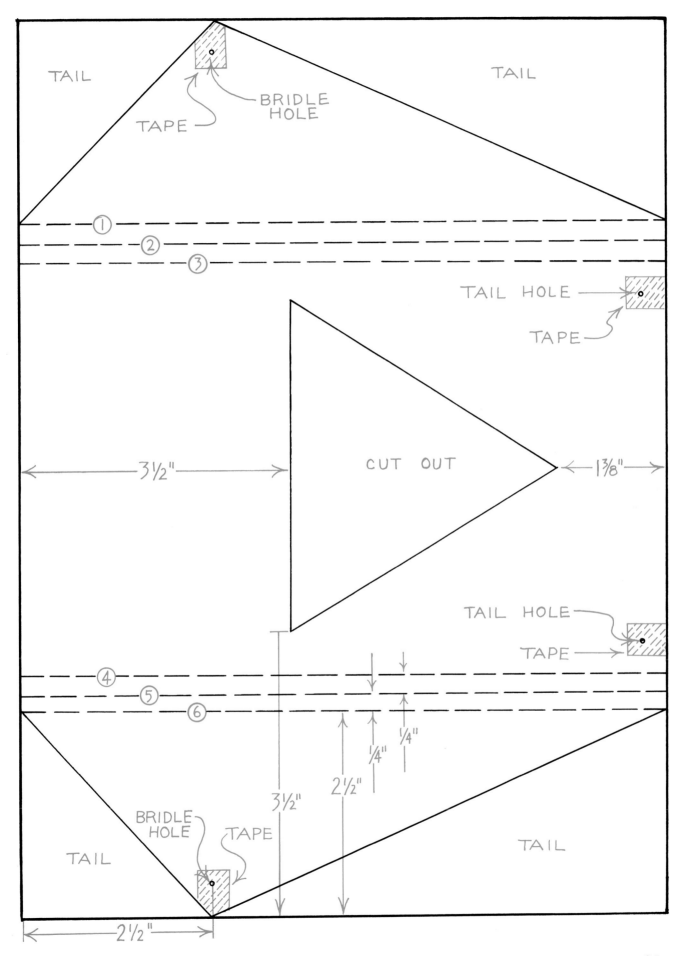

TAIL

TAIL

BRIDLE
HOLE

TAPE

①

②

③

TAIL HOLE

TAPE

CUT OUT

3½"

1⅜"

TAIL HOLE

TAPE

④

⑤

⑥

¼"

¼"

3½"

2½"

BRIDLE
HOLE

TAPE

TAIL

TAIL

2½"

Cut off the four tail pieces and set them aside. Cut out the triangle-shaped hole in the kite's body and discard it.

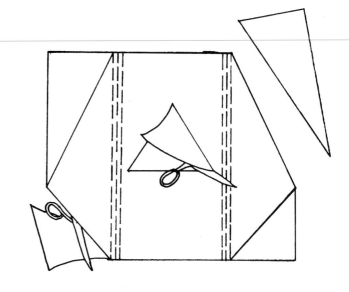

Start by making folds 2 and 5 with the dashed lines outside the creases. Now make folds 1, 3, 4, and 6 in the opposite direction, with the dashed lines inside the creases.

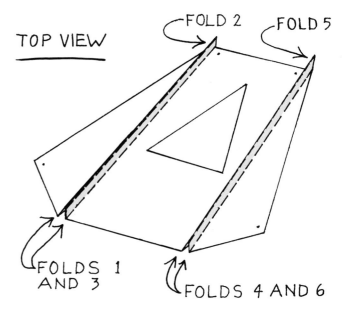

Turn the kite over and hold the folds shut with three pieces of tape along each crease. Folds 1 and 3 will be against each other, and folds 4 and 6 will be against each other. This will create ridges that will give the kite the needed nose-to-tail stiffness.

Place small pieces of tape over the bridle and tail holes and poke the holes with a small pin.

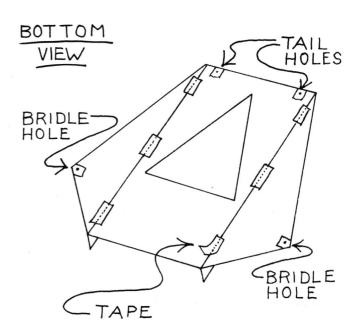

Take the four tail pieces and tape them together to form a narrow rectangle.

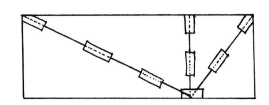

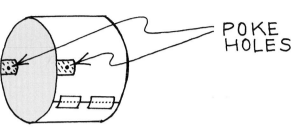

POKE HOLES

Roll this rectangle into a ring and tape the ends together. Place two pieces of tape on the edges of the ring and poke two holes on opposite sides.

Attach two pieces of thread, each about 24 inches long, between the two holes in the ring and the two tail holes in the kite. You might want to attach a small piece of ball chain to the two strands as shown, so that if the tail twists in the wind, it will swivel without tangling the threads.

Tie an 18-inch piece of thread between the two bridle holes. Attach the flying line by twisting the bridle thread around the flying line hook three times, sliding the hook back and forth until the bridle legs are equal. The two ridges formed by the folds should be on the top side of the kite.

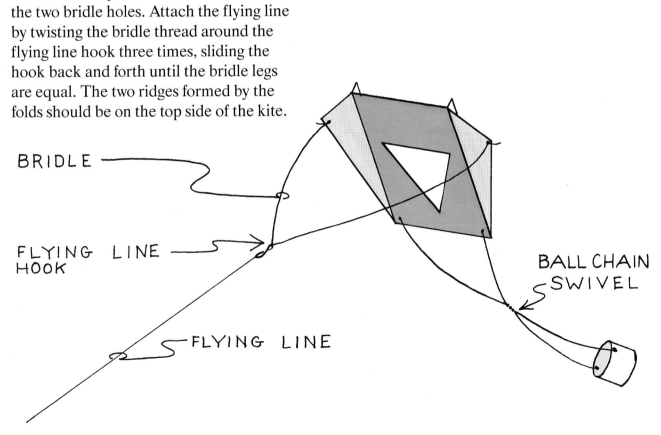

BRIDLE

FLYING LINE HOOK

BALL CHAIN SWIVEL

FLYING LINE

This kite is an excellent flyer that will perform well in light to moderate winds. You might even be able to fly this kite in fresh winds with a larger drouge tail.

8 Half Sheet Kite

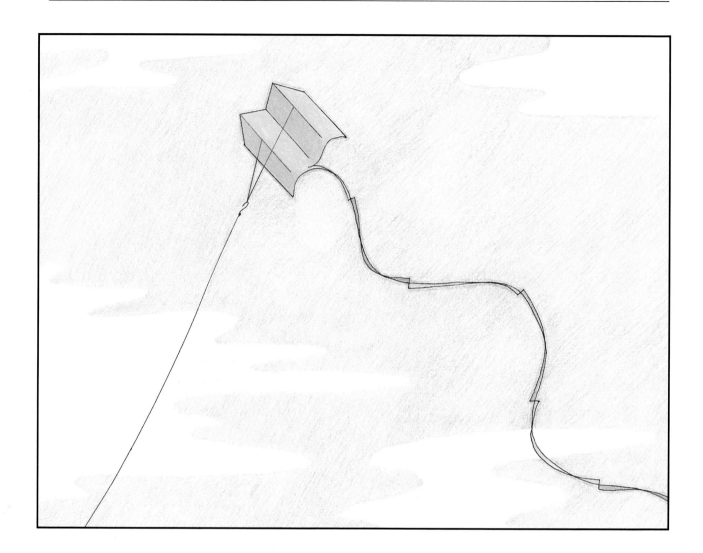

Here is a way to find out how small you can make a kite that will still fly. After making this kite, you may want to try to make some other kites in this book from smaller pieces of paper.

The Half Sheet Kite can be made with regular typing paper and flown on the same thread you have used so far. But the lighter the paper and flying line you use, the better chance this kite has to fly.

Begin by drawing the cut and fold lines from the pattern on the opposite page onto your 8½-by-11-inch piece of paper. Use a ruler to make sure you have the correct measurements. The ″ sign means inches. If you are using a metric ruler, multiply the inch measurements by 2.5 to find centimeters.

Key to lines and symbols

A solid, dark line (——————) shows where to make a *cut*.

A dashed line (— — — — —) shows where to make a *fold*.

A short line at the end of a solid or dashed line (——————) shows where to *stop* cutting or folding.

Blue lines with arrows show *measurements* in inches.

$$\mid\!\longleftarrow\;\;2''\;\;\longrightarrow\!\mid$$

——— 2″ ——→∣   ∣←—

Both examples tell you to make a measurement of two inches between the arrows.

 shows where you will put a piece of tape.

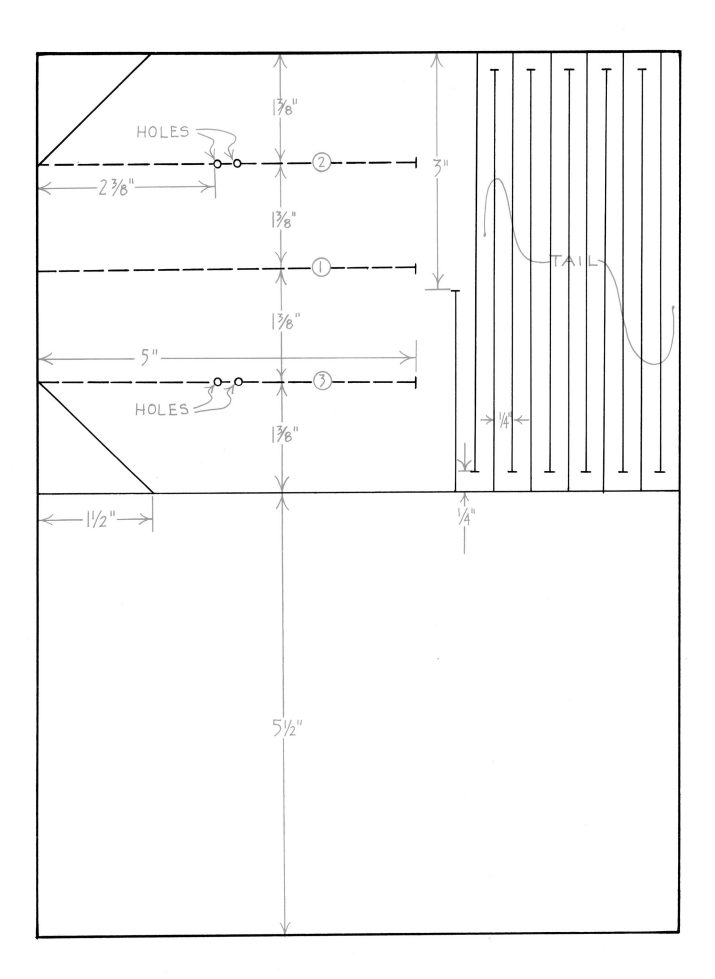

HOLES

2 3/8"

1 3/8"

1 3/8"

1 3/8"

1 3/8"

②

①

③

3"

5"

HOLES

1 1/2"

1/4"

1/4"

TAIL

5 1/2"

Cut off the blank half of your sheet of paper and set it aside. Cut off the two corners at the kite's nose.

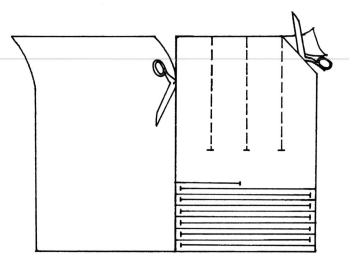

Make each of the three folds. Fold 1 has the dashed line inside the crease. Folds 2 and 3 are made in the opposite direction.

Note that the folds do not go all the way to the tail section. The unfolded portion of the paper will help hold the kite open to the wind. Poke the holes for the bridle inside folds 2 and 3.

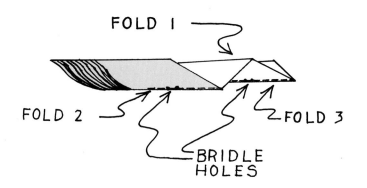

Cut out the tail section of the kite as shown in the diagram. Stop at the small cross lines. Fold the tail so that it hangs down from the kite body. If you make a mistake cutting the tail, you can patch it with a small piece of tape.

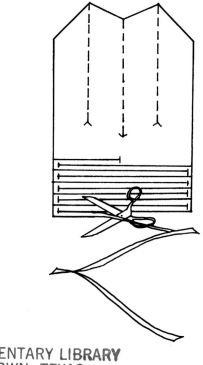

40

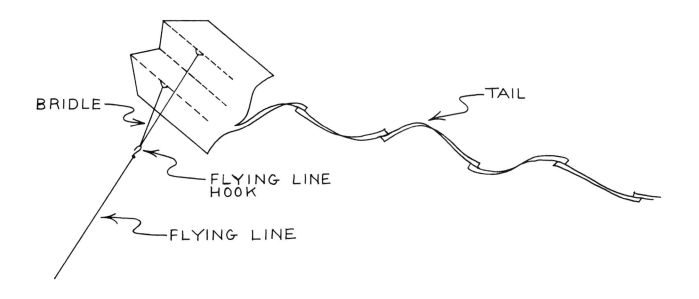

BRIDLE

TAIL

FLYING LINE
HOOK

FLYING LINE

Take a 12-inch piece of thread and tie it from the holes in fold 2 to the holes in fold 3. Wrap the bridle around the hook three times to attach the flying line.

This kite flies well in light and gentle winds. You will find that because the kite is so small, it will not carry much flying line aloft.

There are some special adjustments you can make for better flying results. If the kite has too much lift and circles too much, extend the three folds all the way to the tail end of the kite. If the kite doesn't have enough lift, flatten out the folds. When the wind is just right, you will be surprised at how high this kite can fly.

The Half Sheet Kite is so small that I once folded one up and carried it in my wallet. I wrapped the flying line around an old credit card and took the kite out to fly whenever I had a few spare minutes.

9 Cylindrical Kite

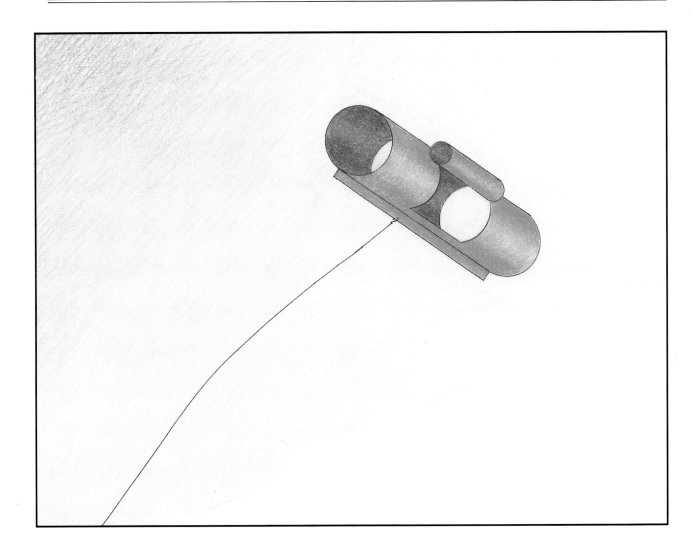

The Cylindrical Kite is a good steady flyer. Some say this kite looks like a jet in flight. The kite has two "thread struts" that provide support against the pressure of the wind.

Begin by drawing the cut and fold lines from the pattern on the opposite page onto your 8½-by-11-inch piece of paper. Use a ruler to make sure you have the correct measurements. The " sign means inches. If you are using a metric ruler, multiply the inch measurements by 2.5 to find centimeters.

Key to lines and symbols

A solid, dark line (————) shows where to make a *cut*.

A dashed line (— — — — —) shows where to make a *fold*.

A short line at the end of a solid or dashed line (————⊣) shows where to *stop* cutting or folding.

Blue lines with arrows show *measurements* in inches.

⊢←——2″——→⊣

————2″——→⊣   ⊢←——

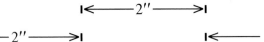

Both examples tell you to make a measurement of two inches between the arrows.

▨ shows where you will put a piece of tape.

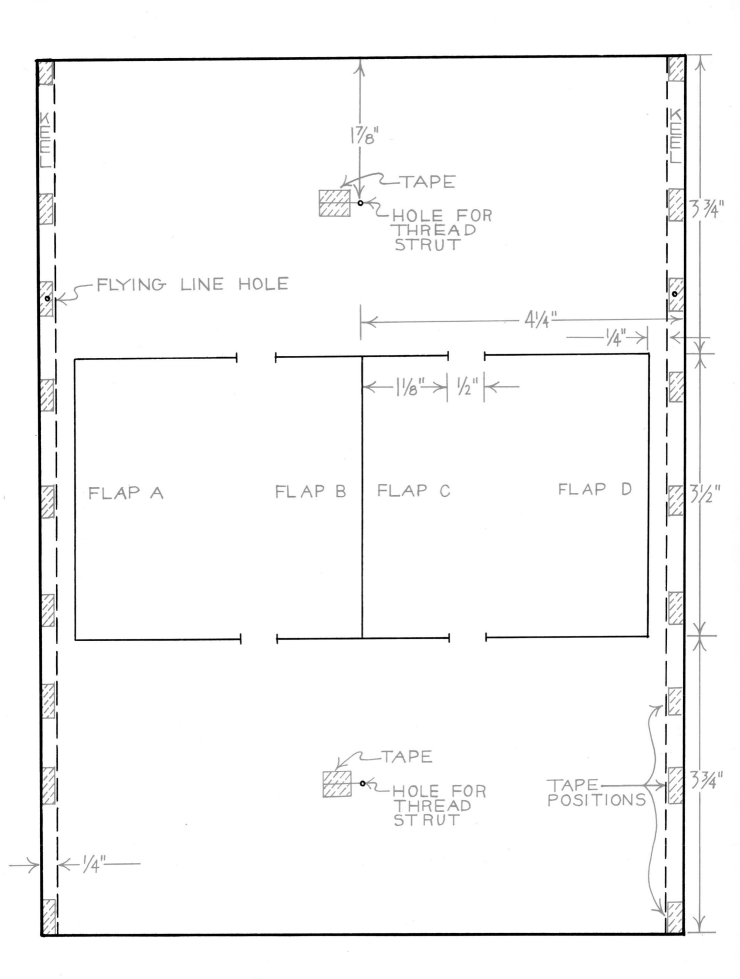

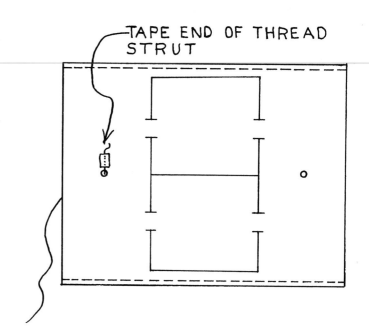

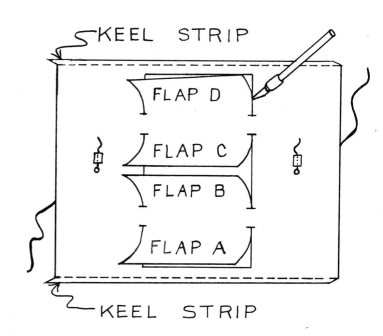

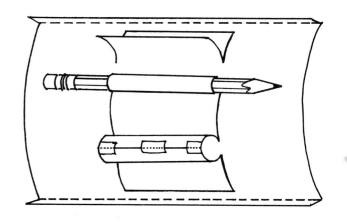

Poke the two "thread strut" holes in the kite with a pin. Take two six-inch pieces of thread and put one into each hole. Tape about an inch of each thread to the kite as shown and let the remainder hang down beneath the kite.

Fold the keel strips with the dashed lines inside the creases. Be sure to make each crease sharp.

Now carefully cut the four flaps. You may wish to use a sharp artist's knife to make the cuts. If you do, protect your tabletop with cardboard or an old magazine.

Roll each flap around a pencil as shown, to make the paper take a curved shape. Now tape the edges of flap A to flap B and the edges of flap C to flap D. This will make two small cylinders.

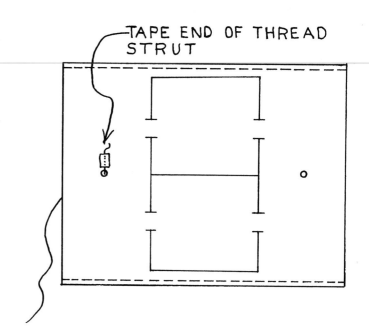

TAPE END OF THREAD STRUT

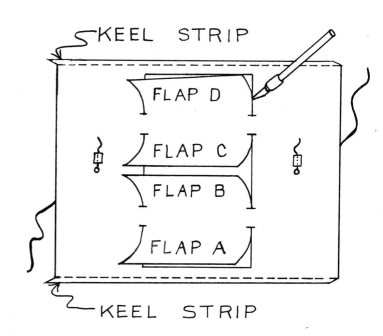

KEEL STRIP

FLAP D

FLAP C

FLAP B

FLAP A

KEEL STRIP

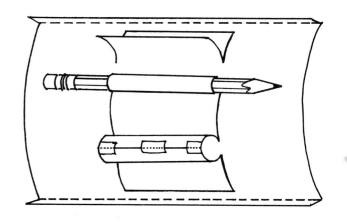

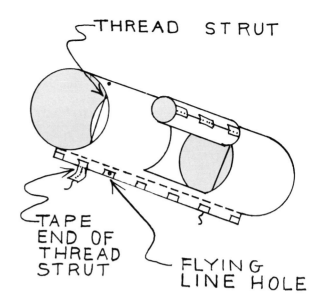

Bring the two keel edges together beneath the kite, curving the entire piece of paper into a cylinder. Tape the keel edges together.

Pull the two thread struts down between the keel edges and tape them in place. The thread struts should be just long enough inside the cylinder to allow the kite to hold a round shape. The struts will help the kite keep its shape against the pressure of the wind.

TAPE
END OF
THREAD
STRUT

FLYING
LINE HOLE

Poke a flying line hole all the way through the keel as marked on the pattern. The flying line hook will attach right to the keel. This kite needs no bridle.

FLYING LINE HOOK

FLYING
LINE

The Cylindrical Kite will fly well in light to moderate winds. It is a steady flyer and requires little adjustment. However, you might want to poke additional holes, ½ inch from the first flying line hole, to adjust the kite's lift if necessary. If you put the flying line hook closer to the nose, you will get less lift and more stability. If you put the hook closer to the tail, you will get more lift and less stability.

This kite was first developed by Alexander Graham Bell when he was studying aerodynamics. The triangle shape gives the kite its stiffness. During World War I, French soldiers added two wings to the kite and flew it like a signal flag. It became known as the French War Kite. Our kite has two small wings between the front and rear cells.

Begin by drawing the cut and fold lines from the pattern on the opposite page onto your 8½-by-11-inch piece of paper. Use a ruler to make sure you have the correct measurements. The ″ sign means inches. If you are using a metric ruler, multiply the inch measurements by 2.5 to find centimeters.

Key to lines and symbols

A solid, dark line (————) shows where to make a *cut*.

A dashed line (— — — — —) shows where to make a *fold*.

A short line at the end of a solid or dashed line (————⊣) shows where to *stop* cutting or folding.

Blue lines with arrows show *measurements* in inches.
⊢←———2″———→⊣

————— 2″ ———→⊣   ⊢←

Both examples tell you to make a measurement of two inches between the arrows.

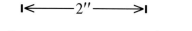 shows where you will put a piece of tape.

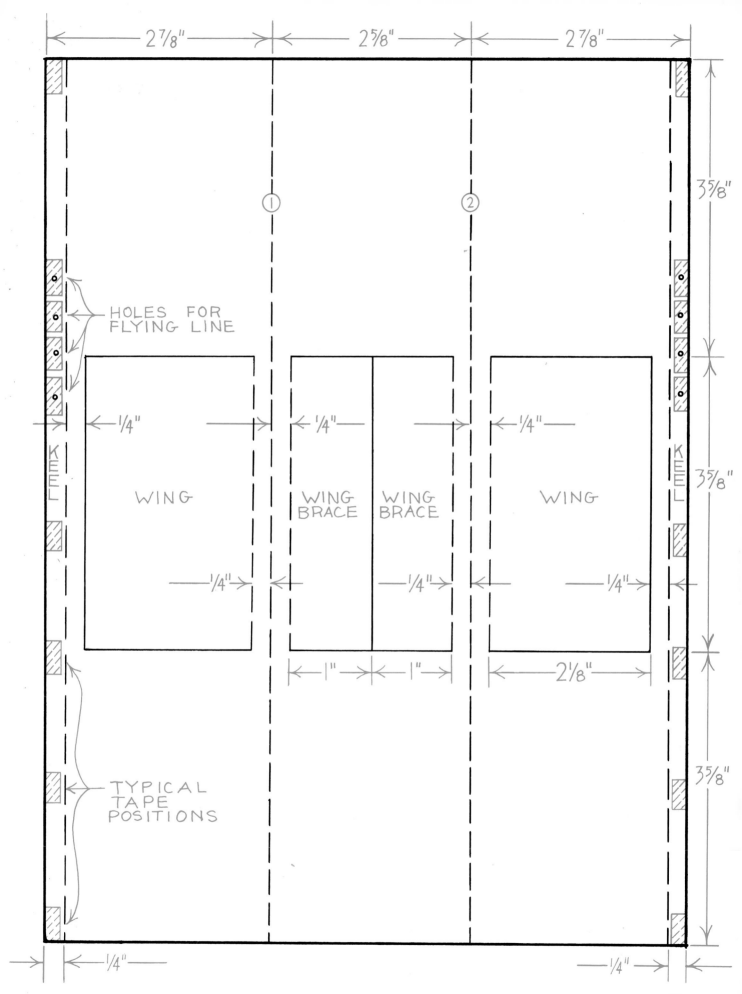

Cut out the wings and wing braces, being careful to stop at the fold lines. You may wish to use a sharp artist's knife to make the cuts. If you do, remember to protect your tabletop.

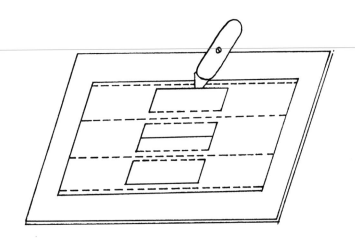

Make folds 1 and 2 with the dashed lines outside the creases. Now fold the keel strips with the dashed lines inside the creases. Make sure all the folds are sharp! Fold the wings and wing braces with the dashed lines inside the creases.

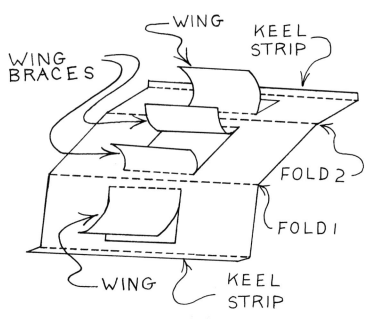

Tape the keel strips together, putting tape over the flying line hook hole positions for reinforcement.

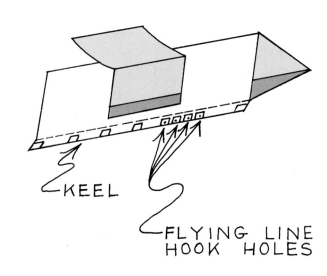

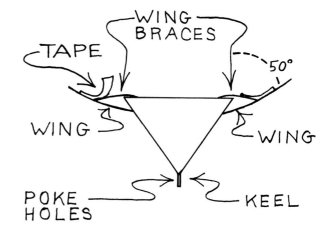

Tape the wing braces to the wings so that the wings stick up at about a 50° angle to the top of the kite. Use tape to attach the braces to each wing.

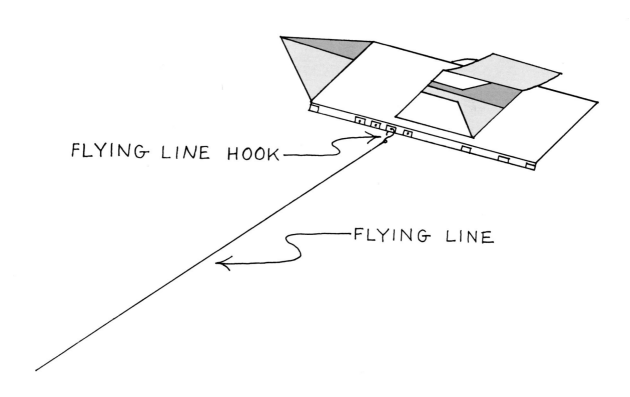

Poke four holes through the keel portion of the kite. Attach the flying line hook directly to one of the four holes and adjust it as necessary. If you put the flying line hook closer to the nose, you will get less lift and more stability. If you put the hook closer to the tail, you will get more lift and less stability.

This kite flies well in light to moderate winds.

This kite lies flat on the wind like a bird in flight. I have seen seagulls fly around this kite to see what kind of strange bird it is!

Begin by drawing the cut and fold lines from the pattern on the opposite page onto your 8½-by-11-inch piece of paper. Use a ruler to make sure you have the correct measurements. The ″ sign means inches. If you are using a metric ruler, multiply the inch measurements by 2.5 to find centimeters.

Note the odd dashed line in the pattern:

━━━ ━ ━ ━ ━ ━ ━ ━ ━ ━

This line shows you how far the edge of each wing is to be rolled.

Key to lines and symbols

A solid, dark line (————) shows where to make a *cut*.

A dashed line (━ ━ ━ ━ ━) shows where to make a *fold*.

A short line at the end of a solid or dashed line (————┤) shows where to *stop* cutting or folding.

Blue lines with arrows show *measurements* in inches.

⊢←———— 2″ ————→⊣

———— 2″ ————→⊣   ⊢←

Both examples tell you to make a measurement of two inches between the arrows.

▨ shows where you will put a piece of tape.

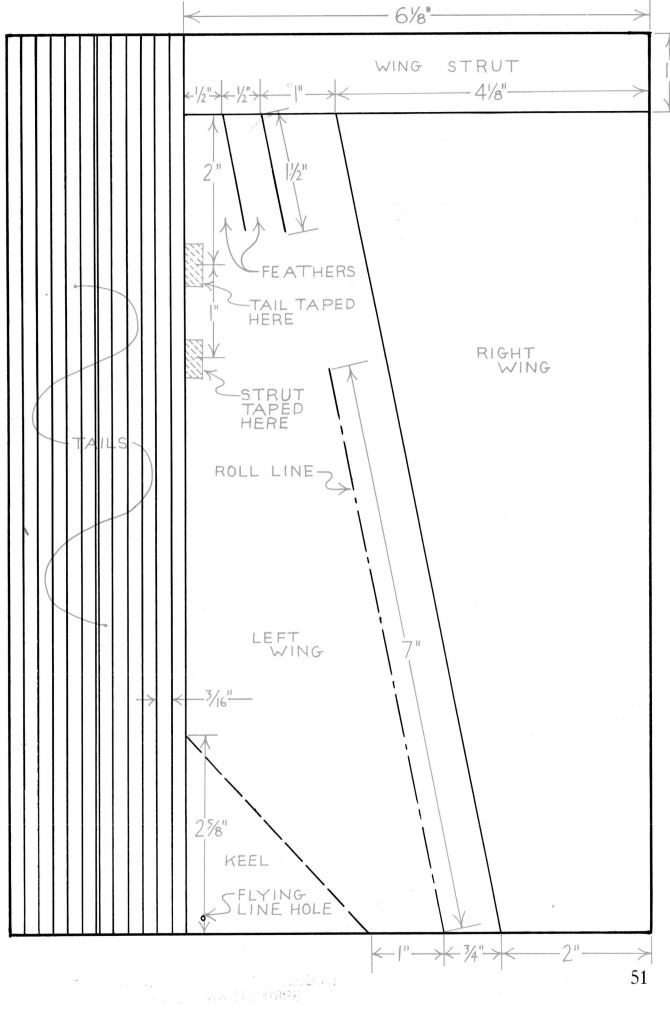

6⅛"

WING STRUT

1"

½" ½" 1" 4⅛"

2"

1½"

FEATHERS

TAIL TAPED HERE

1"

STRUT TAPED HERE

RIGHT WING

TAILS

ROLL LINE

7"

LEFT WING

3/16"

2⅝"

KEEL

FLYING LINE HOLE

1" ¾" 2"

51

Make the cuts to separate the wing strut, tail, and wings as shown.

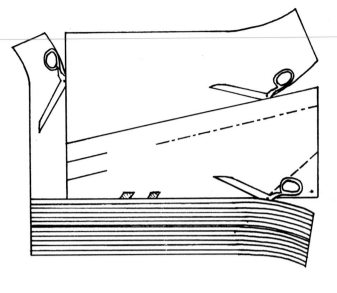

The left and right wings will be mirror images of one another. Using the left wing as a guide, draw the roll line, fold line, feather lines, and the tail and strut positions on the right wing.

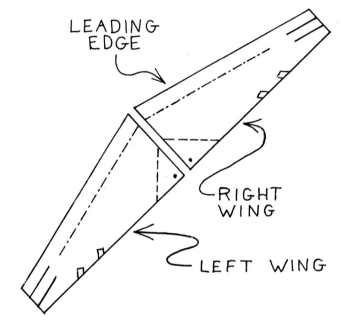

LEADING EDGE

RIGHT WING

LEFT WING

Turn both wings over and roll the leading edge of each around a pencil until you see the roll line on top. Secure the roll with tape.

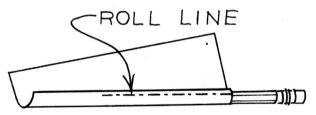

ROLL LINE

Make the corner fold in each wing, with the dashed line outside the fold, to form a keel.

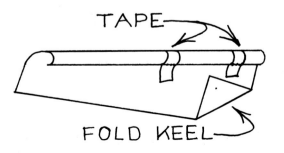

TAPE

FOLD KEEL

Tape the two wings together at the keel. Place a long piece of tape across the top of the wings where they join.

Cut the feathers and curl them upwards. Poke the flying line hook hole with a pin.

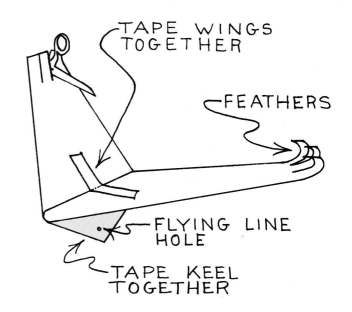

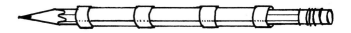

Roll the wing strut around a pencil and secure it with tape. Flatten the ends of the strut and tape them to the wings in the places marked on the pattern. The wings should form a shallow V shape.

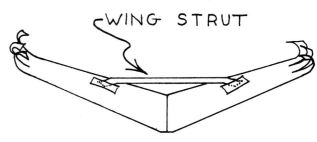

Cut the tail piece into strips and tape these together to form two tails. Tape them to the edge of the wings, near the wing strut.

This kite flies well in light to moderate winds. The tail length is critical and needs to be increased for stronger winds. Because the drag is so low, this kite will fly nearly overhead under the right conditions.

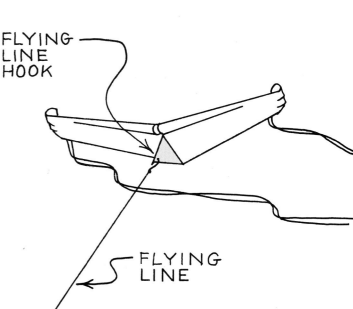

12   A. G. Bell Kite

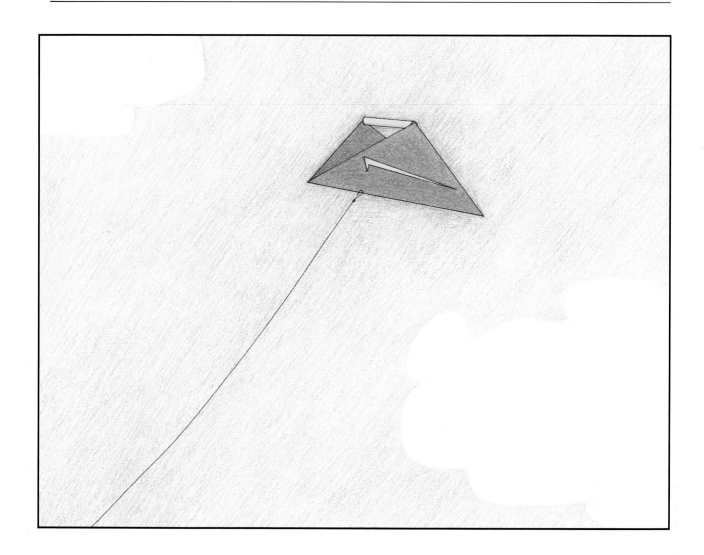

This kite was also developed by Alexander Graham Bell. While working with triangular box kites, Bell discovered that the strongest kite frame possible was shaped like a pyramid. When the frame was covered with fabric on two sides, it flew well without a tail.

Our version has no frame, but it does have a tube strut to help keep it open in the wind.

Begin by drawing the cut and fold lines from the pattern on the opposite page onto your 8½-by-11-inch piece of paper. Use a ruler to make sure you have the correct measurements. The ″ sign means inches. If you are using a metric ruler, multiply the inch measurements by 2.5 to find centimeters.

Key to lines and symbols

A solid, dark line (————) shows where to make a *cut*.

A dashed line (— — — —) shows where to make a *fold*.

A short line at the end of a solid or dashed line (————|) shows where to *stop* cutting or folding.

Blue lines with arrows show *measurements* in inches.

|←————2″————→|

————2″————→| |←

Both examples tell you to make a measurement of two inches between the arrows.

▨ shows where you will put a piece of tape.

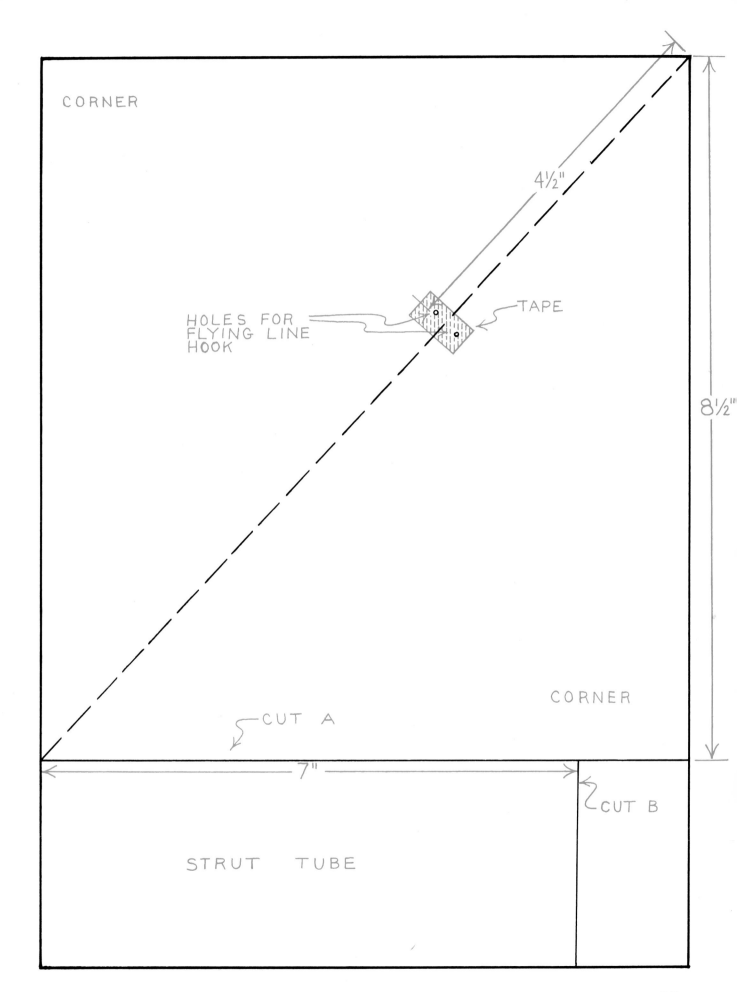

CORNER

4½"

HOLES FOR
FLYING LINE
HOOK

TAPE

8½"

CORNER

CUT A

7"

CUT B

STRUT TUBE

55

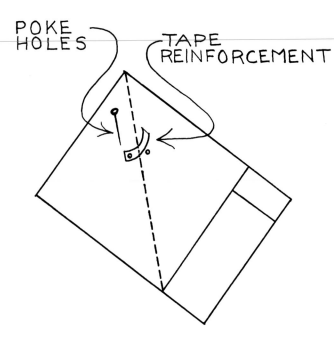

POKE HOLES

TAPE REINFORCEMENT

Place a piece of tape over the holes for the flying line. Poke two holes through the tape with a sharp pin.

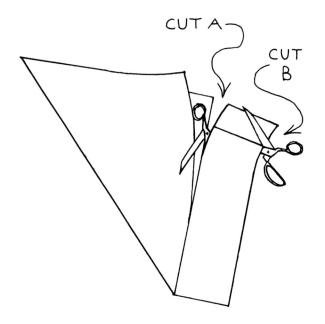

CUT A

CUT B

Make the fold with the tape and the dashed line inside the crease. Make cut A to remove the strut tube strip and shorten it by making cut B at the end.

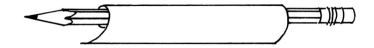

Roll the strut tube around a pencil and let it unroll until it is about ¾ of an inch in diameter. Put pieces of tape along the edges to hold the tube together.

Tuck one corner of the kite into one end of the strut tube and secure it with a long piece of tape. Tuck the other corner into the other end of the strut tube and secure it the same way.

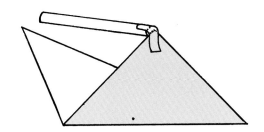

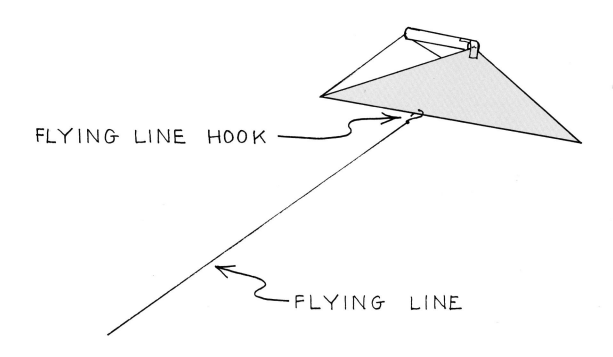

FLYING LINE HOOK

FLYING LINE

Attach the flying line by passing the hook directly through the two holes in the kite's body.

This kite flies best in gentle and moderate winds. It is challenging to fly because it has no tail, although you can add a tail if you wish. You may want to add more holes along the kite's fold so that you can attach the flying line in different places to adjust lift.

13 Four Sheet Kite

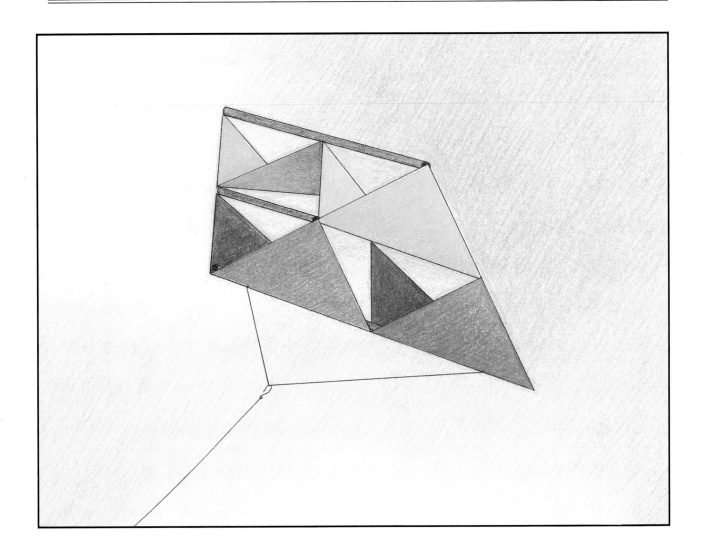

This kite is a further development of Bell's pyramid design. Bell combined pyramid kites and created monsters that contained thousands of small kites. He once lifted a man with one of these monster kites. Our kite will be made out of four smaller kites.

Begin by drawing the cut and fold lines from the pattern on the opposite page onto your 8½-by-11-inch piece of paper. Use a ruler to make sure you have the correct measurements. The ″ sign means inches. If you are using a metric ruler, multiply the inch measurements by 2.5 to find centimeters.

You will need to make four kites, so copy the pattern four times and label the kites 1, 2, 3, and 4.

Key to lines and symbols

A solid, dark line (————) shows where to make a *cut*.

A dashed line (— — — — —) shows where to make a *fold*.

A short line at the end of a solid or dashed line (————|) shows where to *stop* cutting or folding.

Blue lines with arrows show *measurements* in inches.

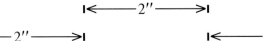

Both examples tell you to make a measurement of two inches between the arrows.

▨ shows where you will put a piece of tape.

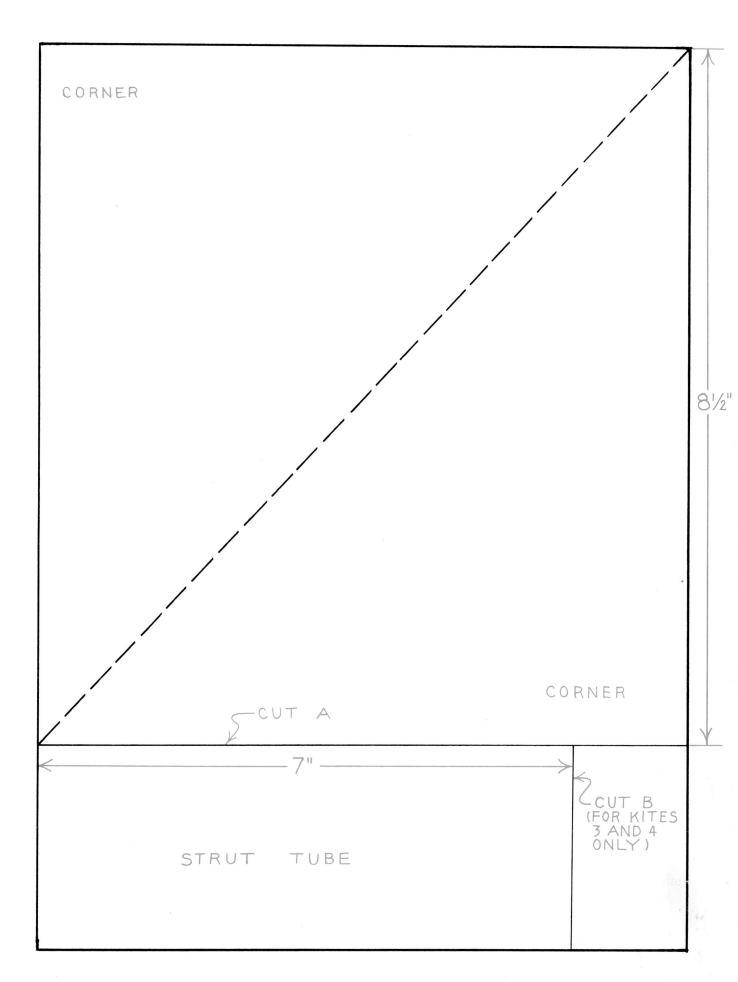

CORNER

8½"

CORNER

CUT A

7"

CUT B
(FOR KITES
3 AND 4
ONLY)

STRUT   TUBE

59

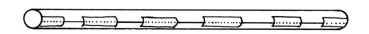

Cut out the pattern for kites 1 and 2, but do not make cut B to shorten the strut pieces.

Instead, tape the strut pieces together lengthwise with a 1½-inch overlap.

Wrap this piece around a pencil and tape it together to form a long strut that is ¾ of an inch in diameter. This will be called the 1-2 strut.

Fold kites 1 and 2 and tape them together at the corners as shown.

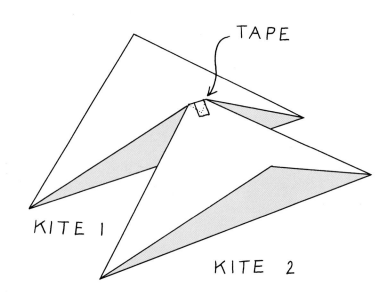

TAPE

KITE 1

KITE 2

With the kites resting on their folds, take the 1-2 strut and tape it across both kites. Tuck the far corners of kites 1 and 2 into the ends of the strut. Secure the strut with tape at the center, where the kites join, and at each end.

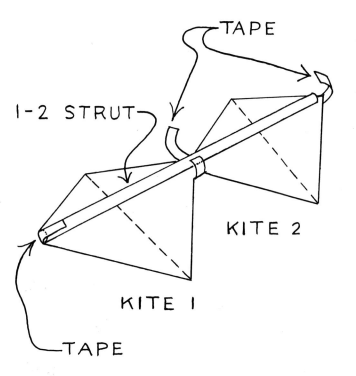

TAPE

1-2 STRUT

KITE 2

KITE 1

TAPE

Build kites 3 and 4, following the directions for the A. G. Bell Kite in the last chapter. Remember to make cut B to shorten the struts. Tape the two kites together with a long piece of tape as shown.

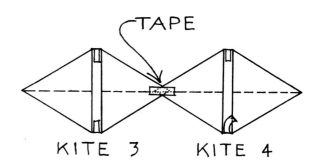

Cut a piece of typing paper in half length-wise, forming two pieces, 4¼ x 11 inches long. Tape the pieces together lengthwise with an overlap of two inches so that the total length of the paper is 20 inches.

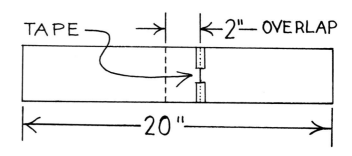

Roll the paper around a pencil or a long stick and tape it closed to form a tube that is about one inch in diameter. This tube is called the keel strut.

Lay the keel strut *inside* kites 3 and 4, along the crease. Tape it in place as shown.

Poke two holes on each side of the tube, five inches from the kite's nose. Poke two more holes on each side of the tube, five inches from the kite's tail.

Tie a 30-inch piece of thread around the keel strut and through the holes on each side. Pass the thread from one set of holes to the other along the bottom of the kite. This thread is the bridle.

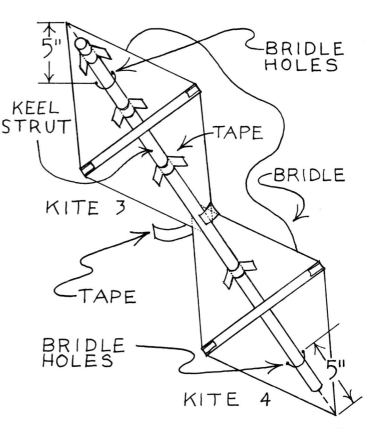

61

Tape kites 1 and 2 sideways on top of kites 3 and 4. Secure them with tape.

Attach the flying line hook by wrapping the bridle thread around the hook three or four times.

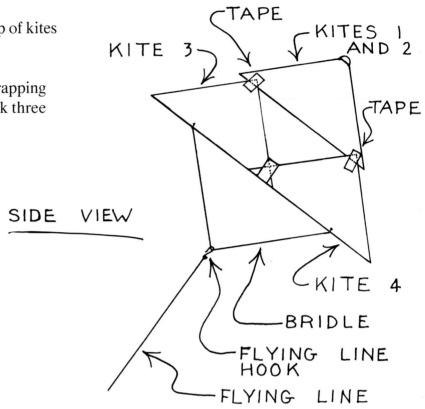

SIDE VIEW

FRONT VIEW

This kite flies well in light to moderate winds. You will be surprised at how strong the pull is and how steadily this kite can fly. You may need to adjust the flying line hook by sliding it toward the nose for less lift or toward the tail for more lift (but less stability).

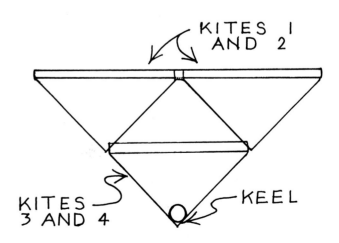

The Sky's the Limit

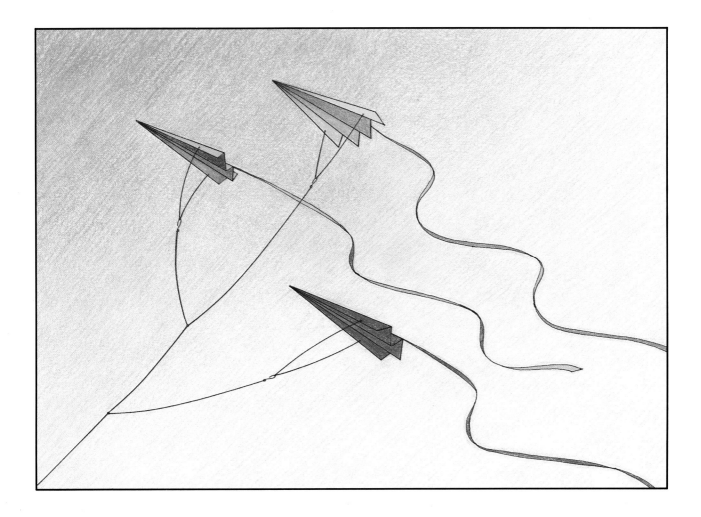

This may be the end of our book, but it is just the beginning of what you can do with your new knowledge about kites.

Make this the starting point for experiments with your own kite designs. Can you make a kite that is smaller than the Half Sheet Kite? What is the best kind of paper and flying line to use for these small kites? Can you make the Arrow Kite larger? Can you modify it for better flying results? Your imagination is the only limit.

How about holding kite-flying contests? Who can make the highest flying kite? Who can make the smallest kite that can still fly? Whose kite is the best decorated? Whose kite lands closest to a certain mark on the ground? Whose kite flies at the highest angle overhead? Which kite is quickest to fly out to a certain length of line? Who can start with a sheet of paper and get a kite flying in the least amount of time? You can think of many more contests yourself.

Kites may also be flown in trains of two, three, or more—with several of the same kind of kite attached to one flying line. Try it yourself. The record is in the hundreds!

You can also go on from here and make or buy kites that use sticks for support. These will be much larger than the kites in this book.

Your interest in aerodynamics may also take you on to books on paper, model, and real airplanes. After all, most of the inventors who helped develop the first airplanes began by studying kites. The Wright brothers' *Flyer* was nothing more than a large box kite.

Finally, any time there is the right wind and you have thread, tape, and a sheet of paper, you can make and fly a kite. Good flying and happy landings!

ABOUT THE AUTHOR

Emery J. Kelly, shown here building a Four Sheet Kite, enjoys teaching young people about kites, airplanes, and aerodynamics. Kelly has worked as a junior high school science teacher and as a weather observer for the United States Air Force. He lives in Arpin, Wisconsin.